THE AUSTRALIAN
Women's Weekly

GLUTEN-FREE
FAMILY FAVOURITES

BB Bounty
BOOKS

CONTENTS

INTRODUCTION
6

BREAKFAST
10

LUNCH
28

DINNER
52

SWEETS
84

SPECIAL OCCASIONS
100

Dr Joanna McMillan

Accredited Practising
Dietitian and Nutritionist
www.drjoanna.com.au www.getlean.com.au

ABOUT
ALLERGIES

If you are picking up this book because you or a family member has a food allergy, you are not alone. The latest Australian data estimates that 1 in 10 infants have a food allergy, most commonly to **raw egg (8.8%)**, followed by **peanuts (3%), cow's milk (2.7%)** and **sesame (0.8%)**. Fortunately, many children grow out of their allergy in the first few years, leaving an estimated 3-5% of older children with an allergy. The food allergies a child is least likely to grow out of are peanuts, tree nuts, seeds and seafood.

If you have a young child with a food allergy, be sure to have an annual allergy review with your clinical immunologist. It makes life much easier to know if your child can now have egg, milk or whatever the offending food may be. Equally you both need to know if the allergy is potentially life-threatening. In adults the rate is much lower, but there remains an estimated 1.3% of people who suffer from a food allergy. The main offender is

peanut, followed by prawn, cow's milk and egg. However, an allergy can develop at any time to pretty much any food. Allergies do not necessarily run in families; if one child has an allergy there is only a slight increase in risk of a sibling also having an allergy. Why some are affected while the majority are not, is a major question in allergy research, and there are not, as yet, any clear answers.

IS FOOD ALLERGY
INCREASING?

Yes, it seems to be. In Australia, hospital admissions for severe allergic reactions have doubled over the last decade, and more people are seeking help from allergy clinics. This rise has been seen in the UK and USA, so we're not alone. Why this is happening is less clear. There are a number of hypotheses, but so far the research has not been able to provide any definitive conclusions. One theory is the 'hygiene hypothesis', which proposes that a lack of exposure to infections, germs, parasites and dirt in general in young childhood affects the development of the immune system. Another theory is the timing of introduction to solid foods. What is clear from the research is that delaying exposure to common allergens does not reduce the incidence of food allergy, and may even increase it. The Australian recommendations for infant feeding are to exclusively breastfeed to around 6 months, at which point solid foods, including potentially allergenic ones, should be introduced. We now have research to show that people who had a cat or dog at home during early childhood are ignificantly less likely to have a pet allergy

later in life. The same may prove to be true of a food allergy. What is crucially important is that if you suspect a food allergy you seek the help of a health-care professional to confirm a diagnosis and help you to create a management care plan. Otherwise you may be unnecessarily restricting your own or your child's diet. With that comes a risk of missing out on specific nutrients, particularly if several foods are avoided. Another source of confusion is the difference between a food allergy and a food intolerance.

WHAT IS A FOOD ALLERGY?

Food allergy results when the immune system reacts to something in the food, usually a protein. The immune system is important in protecting us from disease, but when it reacts improperly to a food it can cause a variety of symptoms ranging from unpleasant to life threatening. In the most serious cases, anaphylactic shock occurs within a few minutes of exposure to the food. The symptoms include a swelling of the face, lips and tongue, weak pulse, dizziness and a difficulty in breathing. If this happens to your child, or you witness this response in someone else, you must seek medical assistance immediately.

This is the type of response that will occur in those with severe peanut allergy if they come into contact with peanut protein. This can be extremely difficult for parents as peanuts are used in many foods that you wouldn't expect. Children have reacted after eating a piece of birthday cake at a party or eating breakfast cereal that was packaged using the same machinery as a nut-containing variety. For this reason it is crucial that those with severe allergies wear an identification bracelet and carry an adrenaline autoinjector (epipen). Shellfish and bee stings are the other most likely candidates for such serious anaphylactic reactions.

With most food allergies, symptoms will appear within 30 minutes of consuming the food – this does have the benefit of making it easier to identify the allergen responsible than is the case for food intolerances.

What is important to note however, is that allergic reactions can escalate after the first or second exposures. It's therefore essential to develop an action plan with your clinical immunologist or allergist.

WHAT IS A FOOD INTOLERANCE?

The definition of a food intolerance is 'a reproducible, unpleasant (adverse), non-psychological reaction to a specific food or food ingredient'. In other words, the immune system is not involved. While many symptoms can be similar to a food allergy (although not as serious as an anaphylactic reaction), diagnosis can be much more difficult. This is due, in part, to the fact that symptoms may not appear until many hours after consuming the food. For example, one common food intolerance is milk and is due to a lack of the enzyme lactase that breaks down the sugar (lactose) in milk. Without this enzyme the milk sugar enters the colon undigested where it is fermented by the resident bacteria. Other common food intolerances are to wheat, dairy products, eggs, fish or shellfish, caffeine or soy products. The symptoms produced are similar to the less severe allergic reactions listed on the page opposite.

TYPICAL REACTIONS TO A
FOOD ALLERGY OR INTOLERANCE

Reactions can affect four main areas:

● The gastrointestinal system: causing abdominal cramps, nausea, vomiting and/or diarrhoea. Nuts are often the culprit food where immediate effects take place. In chronic diarrhoea, most often in children, wheat, milk or soy products may be the cause.

● The skin: causing the eruption of hives or for some, a swelling of the lips, ears, eyes and face. Eczema may also be due to a food allergy, but there are many other causes so it is important to seek proper medical advice before omitting foods from your or your child's diet.

● The respiratory system: causing a runny or stuffy nose. Although many people believe their asthma is linked to a food allergy, allergists consider this unlikely and airborne substances, such as dust mites, are the more likely offenders.

● The vascular system: causing a number of different symptoms from migraine headaches to numbness, flushing and dizziness. The latter may be caused by ingesting fairly large doses of mono-sodium glutamate (MSG) and is often referred to as Chinese restaurant syndrome due to their frequent use of this additive. However, the symptoms are short term and do not involve IgE (allergic) responses – the sign of a classic allergy. They don't require medical treatment and it usually just clears up on its own. If someone suspects this is the case for them, avoiding excess MSG is wise. If you suffer from frequent migraines that cannot be explained by any other cause, you may benefit from experimenting with cutting out these foods from your

diet: strong cheeses, red wine, champagne, chocolate, citrus fruit, gluten and cured meats such as bacon, salami, hot dogs and ham.

The difficulty with food allergies and intolerances is that they can be difficult to identify – the symptoms are usually non-specific and can be attributed to many other causes. Many people unnecessarily omit food from their diet believing they are intolerant to them. This may not be a problem if it is only one or two foods, but where these foods are not adequately replaced, or numerous foods are omitted, the individual is at risk of nutrient deficiencies.

Most commonly, people are advised to give up wheat and dairy products. This is not as easy as it sounds and, for the few individuals who are affected, the help of a dietitian is warranted to ensure the resulting diet is nutritionally sound. However, the vast majority of people do not need to give up these foods. Wheat and dairy foods have many benefits and need only be avoided by those with a true allergy or intolerance. The fact only 40% of people claiming to have a food intolerance actually show symptoms when tested is testament to the level of non-essential food restrictions we have placed on ourselves.

Better food labelling has made things easier for those living with a food allergy. Learn what to look for in the ingredient lists – in Australia the nine most common food allergens must be declared on the packaging. You'll usually find them highlighted in bold in the ingredients list.

BREAKFAST

It's the most important meal of the day, but breakfast doesn't have to be boring! Literally meaning 'break fast' because it refuels the body after the overnight period, breakfast replenishes the body of glucose and essential nutrients and has been shown to improve concentration. From lazy brunches to midweek meals, these recipes will help you to start your day the right way.

BUCKWHEAT WAFFLES WITH GOLDEN SYRUP

Perfect for lazy Sunday mornings, this decadent breakfast treat is the ideal addition for a delicious gluten-free brunch.

INGREDIENTS

⅓ cup (60g) dairy-free spread

2 tablespoons caster (superfine) sugar

3 eggs, separated

⅓ cup (45g) gluten-free plain (all-purpose) flour

⅓ cup (50g) buckwheat flour

⅓ cup (50g) 100% corn (maize) cornflour (cornstarch)

1 cup (135g) gluten-free self-raising flour

1 teaspoon gluten-free baking powder

1 teaspoon bicarbonate of soda (baking soda)

½ teaspoon salt

½ teaspoon ground cinnamon

1½ cups (375ml) soy milk

1½ teaspoons white vinegar

cooking-oil spray

250g (8 ounces) strawberries, sliced

⅔ cup (230g) golden syrup

METHOD

1 Beat dairy-free spread and sugar in a medium bowl with an electric mixer until light and fluffy. Beat in egg yolks, one at a time.

2 Beat egg whites in a small bowl with an electric mixer until soft peaks form. Gently fold egg whites into egg-yolk mixture.

3 Fold sifted dry ingredients, soy milk and vinegar into egg mixture until the mix just comes together. (Do not over mix the waffle mixture; it may look slightly curdled at this stage.)

4 Spray a heated waffle iron with oil; pour ½ cup batter over bottom element of waffle iron. Close iron; cook waffle for about 3 minutes or until browned both sides and crisp. Transfer waffle to a plate; cover to keep warm.

5 Repeat step 4 to make a total of 6 waffles. Serve waffles with sliced strawberries and drizzled with golden syrup.

INFO				SERVES 6
PREP + COOK TIME 45 MINUTES				
HEALTH FACTOR	GLUTEN FREE	DAIRY FREE	NUT FREE	

FAT	ENERGY	CARB	PROTEIN	FIBRE
11g (2.5g sat)	1669kJ (399 cal)	78.2g	6.4g	0.8g

PER SERVING

TOP TIPS

If you don't have a waffle iron, you can cook the waffles in a jaffle iron. Waffles can be frozen in an airtight container for up to 3 months; reheat in a moderate oven for about 15 minutes or until warmed through. You can use your favourite dairy-free milk in this recipe.

HAM & GREEN ONION FRITTERS

INGREDIENTS

250g (8 ounces) red grape tomatoes

1 teaspoon balsamic vinegar

1½ tablespoons olive oil

1 cup (135g) gluten-free self-raising flour

¾ cup (180ml) soy milk

250g (8 ounces) gluten-free shaved ham, chopped finely

4 green onions (scallions), sliced thinly

1 large avocado (320g), chopped coarsely

METHOD

1 Preheat oven to 200°C/400°F.

2 Place tomatoes on an oven tray; drizzle with vinegar and 1 teaspoon of the oil. Season. Roast for 15 minutes or until tomatoes just soften.

3 Sift flour into a large bowl. Gradually add milk, in batches, stirring after each addition. Add ham and green onion; stir to combine. Season.

4 Heat remaining oil in a large non-stick frying pan over medium heat. Spoon ¼-cups of batter into pan; cook for 2½ minutes each side or until golden brown and cooked through. Repeat with remaining batter to make a total of eight fritters.

5 Serve fritters with avocado and tomatoes.

INFO				SERVES 4
PREP + COOK TIME 20 MINUTES				
HEALTH FACTOR	GLUTEN FREE	DAIRY FREE	NUT FREE	

FAT	ENERGY	CARB	PROTEIN	FIBRE
24.8g (5.6g sat)	1822kJ (435 cal)	31.5g	20.1g	2.8g

PER SERVING

GRILLED EGGS WITH SPICED FENNEL & SPINACH

You need an ovenproof frying pan for this recipe as the pan goes under the grill. If you don't have one, cover the pan handle with a few layers of foil to protect it from the heat.

INGREDIENTS

1 tablespoon olive oil

1 clove garlic, crushed

1 fresh small red thai (serrano) chilli, sliced finely

1 small fennel bulb (200g), trimmed, sliced finely

200g (6½ ounces) baby corn, halved

100g (3 ounces) baby spinach leaves

4 eggs

2 tablespoons finely grated parmesan

4 slices gluten-free bread (180g), toasted

METHOD

1 Preheat grill (broiler) to high.

2 Heat oil in a large ovenproof non-stick frying pan over medium heat; cook garlic, chilli, fennel and corn, stirring occasionally, for 5 minutes or until fennel is soft. Add spinach; cook, stirring, for 1 minute or until spinach has wilted.

3 Make four holes in the spinach mixture; break one egg into each hole. Sprinkle with parmesan.

4 Place under grill for 2 minutes or until eggs are cooked as desired.

5 Serve eggs and spinach mixture with toast.

INFO				SERVES 4

PREP + COOK TIME 20 MINUTES				
HEALTH FACTOR	GLUTEN FREE	NUT FREE		

FAT	ENERGY	CARB	PROTEIN	FIBRE
18.3g (4.9g sat)	581kJ (378 cal)	28g	21.6g	7.2g

PER SERVING

BUTTERMILK PANCAKES WITH LEMON & SUGAR

Add a touch of something special to the breakfast table with these deliciously sweet gluten-free pancakes.

INGREDIENTS

1 cup (135g) gluten-free self-raising flour

¼ cup (35g) gluten-free plain (all-purpose) flour

1 tablespoon caster (superfine) sugar

1 cup (250ml) buttermilk

½ cup (125ml) milk

2 eggs

20g (¾ ounce) butter, melted

½ cup (110g) caster (superfine) sugar

1 medium lemon (140g), cut into wedges

METHOD

1 Sift flours and sugar into a medium bowl. Gradually whisk in combined buttermilk, milk and eggs until smooth. Stand for 5 minutes.

2 Heat a medium heavy-based frying pan over medium heat; brush with a little melted butter. Reduce heat to low, pour 2 tablespoons of batter into pan; cook until bubbles appear on the surface and top appears to dry out a little. Turn pancakes; cook until browned lightly. Remove from pan; cover to keep warm. Repeat with remaining butter and batter to make 12 pancakes, wiping out pan between batches.

3 Serve pancakes topped with sugar and lemon wedges.

INFO				SERVES 4
PREP + COOK TIME 20 MINUTES				
HEALTH FACTOR	GLUTEN FREE	YEAST FREE	NUT FREE	
FAT 9.3g (5.2g sat)	ENERGY 1677kJ (401 cal)	CARB 72.3g	PROTEIN 7.7g	FIBRE 0g

PER SERVING

• TOP TIPS

Make pancakes just before serving. Serve pancakes with jam and cream, butter and brown sugar, or lemon butter, if you like.

4 WAYS WITH CEREALS & GRAINS

QUINOA PORRIDGE WITH GRAPES & PISTACHIOS

Place 1 cup rinsed, drained white quinoa and 3 cups water in a large saucepan; bring to the boil. Reduce heat to low; cook, covered, for 10 minutes. Add 1 cup skim milk; cook, covered, for a further 5 minutes or until quinoa is tender. Stir in 2 medium coarsely grated pink lady apples and 100g (3oz) halved seedless red grapes. Serve porridge topped with another 100g (3oz) halved seedless red grapes and $\frac{1}{3}$ cup coarsely chopped roasted pistachios; drizzle with 2 tablespoons honey.

INFO   SERVES 4

PREP + COOK TIME 25 MINUTES

GRANOLA WITH PLUMS & VANILLA YOGHURT

Preheat oven to 150°C/300°F. Line a large oven tray with baking paper. Combine 1 cup each of gluten-free cornflakes, rice-bran cereal and puffed rice and $\frac{1}{3}$ cup pepitas and sunflower seed mix in a large bowl. Drizzle with $\frac{1}{4}$ cup honey and 1 tablespoon vegetable oil; sprinkle with $\frac{1}{2}$ teaspoon ground cinnamon. Toss to combine. Spread on tray. Bake, turning occasionally, for 20 minutes or until lightly golden. Stir through $\frac{1}{2}$ cup thickly sliced dried figs and $\frac{1}{3}$ cup sultanas; cool. Divide into serving bowls; drizzle with 700g (1½ lb) vanilla soy yoghurt and top with 2 plums in natural syrup.

INFO   SERVES 4

PREP + COOK TIME 40 MINUTES (+ COOLING)

MAPLE-GLAZED PUFFED CORN

Preheat oven to 180°C/350°F. Grease and line a large baking tray with baking paper. Combine 6 cups puffed corn and 1 cup maple syrup on tray; toss to coat. Bake, uncovered, stirring occasionally, for 20 minutes or until golden brown. Cool on tray. Serve with ½ cup vanilla soy yoghurt. Store in an airtight container in the fridge for up to 3 months. Serve in little noodle boxes or paper cones, if you like. This recipe can also be an afternoon snack.

BIRCHER MUESLI WITH BLUEBERRIES

Combine 2 cups gluten-free quick oats, 1 large coarsely grated green apple, ½ cup apple juice, ⅓ cup orange juice, ½ cup vanilla soy yoghurt, 1 tablespoon caster (superfine) sugar, 1 tablespoon finely grated orange rind, ½ teaspoon ground cinnamon and ¼ teaspoon ground cardamom in a large bowl. Cover with plastic wrap; refrigerate for 1 hour or overnight. Add 125g (4oz) blueberries; stir to combine. Top with extra orange rind to serve, if you like.

INFO   SERVES 4

PREP + COOK TIME   30 MINUTES (+ COOLING)

INFO   SERVES 4

PREP TIME (+ STANDING)   15 MINUTES

BREAKFAST WRAPS

These delicious breaky wraps are not only gluten-free, but are also yeast, dairy and nut-free, making them the perfect all-rounder.

INGREDIENTS

cooking-oil spray

4 eggs

4 rindless bacon slices (260g)

1 tablespoon dairy-free spread

150g (4½ ounces) button mushrooms, sliced thinly

60g (2 ounces) baby spinach leaves

2 tablespoons gluten-free barbecue sauce

GLUTEN-FREE WRAPS

2 eggs

1 cup (135g) gluten-free self-raising flour

⅓ cup (50g) buckwheat flour

⅓ cup (45g) gluten-free plain (all-purpose) flour

⅓ cup (50g) 100% corn (maize) cornflour (cornstarch)

1½ teaspoons salt

⅔ cup (160ml) soy milk

⅔ cup (160ml) water

METHOD

1 Make gluten-free wraps.

2 Spray a medium frying pan with oil; cook eggs over medium heat. Transfer to a plate; cover to keep warm.

3 Cook bacon in the same pan until crisp; transfer to the plate, cover to keep warm. Melt dairy-free spread in same heated pan; cook mushrooms over medium heat for 5 minutes or until just softened.

4 Divide spinach, mushrooms and bacon between wraps; drizzle with barbecue sauce; top with egg. Season. Roll wraps to serve.

GLUTEN-FREE WRAPS

Beat eggs in a small bowl with an electric mixer until thick and pale. Stir in the sifted dry ingredients, and the combined milk and water, alternately, stirring until just combined; do not over mix. Heat a flat sandwich press until light indicates it is ready to use; spray with oil. Pour ⅓ cup of mixture in a circle shape onto press; fully close lid and cook for 2 minutes or until golden brown. Transfer to a plate. Repeat to make a total of four wraps.

INFO				SERVES 4
PREP + COOK TIME 50 MINUTES				

HEALTH FACTOR	GLUTEN FREE	DAIRY FREE	NUT FREE	YEAST FREE

FAT	ENERGY	CARB	PROTEIN	FIBRE
20.6g (6.5g sat)	2148kJ (513 cal)	66.6g	26.1g	1.4g

PER WRAP

TOP TIPS

You need a sandwich press with two flat elements for this recipe. If you don't have one, spread $1/3$ cup of batter into a round shape in a heated large frying pan; cook both sides until brown and cooked through.

OMELETTE WITH ASPARAGUS & MINT

INGREDIENTS

2 baby new potatoes (80g), cut into 5mm (¼-inch) cubes

340g (11 ounces) asparagus, trimmed

2 cups (240g) frozen peas

4 eggs

½ cup coarsely chopped fresh mint leaves

2 tablespoons olive oil

2 slices gluten-free bread (90g), toasted

METHOD

1 Cook potato in a small saucepan of boiling water for 3 minutes. Add asparagus and peas; cook a further 1 minute or until asparagus is bright green and potato is tender. Drain. When cool enough to handle, cut the asparagus in half; finely chop the stem ends.

2 Lightly whisk eggs in a medium bowl; stir in potato, peas, mint and chopped asparagus ends.

3 Heat 2 teaspoons of the oil in a small non-stick frying pan on high; cook a quarter of the egg mixture, for about 2 minutes, pulling in the egg with a spatula to help it cook quickly. Fold over; slide onto a warm serving plate. Repeat with remaining oil and egg mixture to make a total of four omelettes.

4 Serve omelettes with remaining asparagus and toast.

INFO				SERVES 4
PREP + COOK TIME 20 MINUTES				
HEALTH FACTOR	GLUTEN FREE	DAIRY FREE	NUT FREE	
FAT 15.8g (3.4g sat)	ENERGY 1400kJ (335 cal)	CARB 27.7g	PROTEIN 16.3g	FIBRE 8.8g

PER SERVING

• TOP TIPS

If you are pressed for time, make one big omelette in a medium frying pan. You can change the filling depending on the seasonal vegetables available - try adding pumpkin or broccolini.

SAUSAGE, MUSHROOM & TOMATO ROLLS

INGREDIENTS

4 small roma (egg) tomatoes (240g), halved

400g (12½ ounces) button or cup mushrooms, sliced thickly

1 clove garlic, chopped finely

1 tablespoon olive oil

2 teaspoons balsamic vinegar

cooking-oil spray

8 gluten-free beef chipolata sausages (400g)

80g (2½ ounces) baby spinach leaves

4 gluten-free, wheat-free, egg-free bread rolls (200g), split, toasted

METHOD

1 Preheat oven to 150°C/300°F.

2 Combine tomato, mushrooms and garlic in a medium roasting pan, drizzle with oil and vinegar; toss to coat, season. Bake for 30 minutes or until tomatoes begin to soften. Cool slightly.

3 Spray a large frying pan with oil; heat over medium heat. Cook sausages until golden brown and cooked through. Cool slightly; slice thickly lengthways.

4 To serve, sandwich spinach, tomato, mushrooms and sausage between bread roll halves.

INFO   SERVES 4

PREP + COOK TIME 40 MINUTES				
HEALTH FACTOR	GLUTEN FREE	DAIRY FREE	NUT FREE	EGG FREE
FAT 24.9g (14.3g sat)	ENERGY 2398kJ (573 cal)	CARB 36.7g	PROTEIN 25.4g	FIBRE 6.8g

PER SERVING

CRUMPETS WITH RHUBARB COMPOTE

There's something comforting about crumpets, and while the homemade variety may not have as many holes, they're just as tasty as store bought ones.

You need 4 egg rings for this recipe.

INGREDIENTS

1½ cups (375ml) warm water

2 teaspoons (7g) dry yeast

1½ cups (200g) gluten-free plain (all-purpose) flour

½ cup (75g) 100% corn (maize) cornflour (cornstarch)

1½ teaspoons salt

2 tablespoons brown sugar

¼ cup (60ml) soy milk

1 tablespoon dairy-free spread

RHUBARB COMPOTE

300g (9½ ounces) trimmed rhubarb, cut into 4cm (1½-inch) lengths

1 cinnamon stick

1 tablespoon finely grated orange rind

⅓ cup (80ml) orange juice

¼ cup (55g) caster (superfine) sugar

INFO   SERVES 8

PREP + COOK TIME 1 HOUR (+ STANDING)				
HEALTH FACTOR	GLUTEN FREE	DAIRY FREE	NUT FREE	EGG FREE

FAT	ENERGY	CARB	PROTEIN	FIBRE
1.9 g (0.4g sat)	807kJ (193 cal)	41g	2.1g	1g

PER SERVING

METHOD

1 Combine ¼ cup of the water and all the yeast in a small bowl. Cover; stand in a warm place for 10 minutes or until mixture is frothy.

2 Sift flours into a medium bowl; stir in salt and sugar. Make a well in the centre; gradually whisk in the milk and the remaining water until combined. Add the yeast mixture; whisk until smooth. Cover; stand in a warm place for 30 minutes or until mixture has risen slightly.

3 Melt dairy-free spread.

4 Heat a large heavy-based frying pan over low heat. Brush a little of the melted spread over base of pan and around the insides of four egg rings; place rings in pan.

5 Pour 2 tablespoons of batter into each ring; cook, uncovered, until bubbles appear and the surface is a little dry. Using egg slide, turn rings; cook for 1 minute or until crumpets are cooked through. Remove from pan; cover to keep warm. Repeat to make 16 crumpets in total, brushing pan and rings with melted spread between each batch.

6 Meanwhile, make rhubarb compote.

7 Serve crumpets topped with compote.

RHUBARB COMPOTE

Combine ingredients in a medium saucepan over medium heat; simmer, covered, for 5 minutes or until rhubarb is tender.

RASPBERRY & BANANA BREAD

What could be more heavenly than waking up to the aroma of freshly baked banana bread? Just slice, lightly toast and enjoy.

You need 3 large overripe bananas (690g) for the mashed banana in this recipe.

INGREDIENTS

1½ cups (350g) mashed banana

½ cup (125ml) vegetable oil

½ cup (125ml) soy milk

2½ cups (335g) gluten-free self-raising flour

1¼ cups (275g) firmly packed brown sugar

½ teaspoon bicarbonate of soda (baking soda)

1 cup (80g) desiccated coconut

1 cup (150g) frozen raspberries

20g (¾ ounce) dairy-free spread

1 large banana (230g), sliced thickly diagonally

⅓ cup (115g) golden syrup

METHOD

1 Preheat oven to 180°C/375°F. Grease a 10cm x 20cm (4-inch x 8-inch) loaf pan; line base and long sides with baking paper, extending the paper 5cm (2 inches) over the sides.

2 Combine mashed banana, oil and milk in a small bowl.

3 Combine sifted flour, sugar and bicarbonate of soda with coconut in a large bowl. Make a well in the centre. Pour banana mixture into well; stir to combine. Fold in raspberries until just combined. Spoon mixture into pan; smooth the surface.

4 Bake bread about 1¼ hours or until a skewer inserted into the centre comes out clean. Stand bread in pan for 5 minutes before turning, top-side up, onto a wire rack to cool.

5 Melt dairy-free spread in a large frying pan over high heat, add sliced banana; cook 1 minute each side or until caramelised. Thickly slice bread, top with banana; drizzle with golden syrup.

TOP TIPS

Use your favourite dairy-free milk for this recipe. You can replace the raspberries with blueberries or chopped pear, or leave the fruit out altogether. Cut the bread into portion-sized pieces and freeze in an airtight container for up to 3 months. The bread can be toasted to serve.

INFO					SERVES 4
PREP + COOK TIME 1¾ HOURS (+ STANDING)					
HEALTH FACTOR	GLUTEN FREE	DAIRY FREE	NUT FREE	YEAST FREE	EGG FREE
FAT 23g (7.4g sat)	ENERGY 246kJ (588 cal)	CARB 93.4g	PROTEIN 2.7g	FIBRE 4.3g	

PER SERVING

LUNCH

Whether you need something portable to take into the office, pack as a picnic, or to serve up to impress friends and family over an afternoon of feasting, these delicious lunch recipes are super-tasty and free of gluten. From healthy salads, to wraps and rolls, there's something here for the whole family and every lunchtime occassion.

SALMON & QUINOA SALAD

INGREDIENTS

1 cup (200g) white quinoa

3 cups (750ml) water

200g (6½ ounces) snow peas, trimmed, sliced thinly lengthways

1 lebanese cucumber (130g), halved lengthways, sliced thinly crossways

½ cup loosely packed small fresh mint leaves

¼ cup (60ml) lemon juice

2 tablespoons olive oil

150g (4½ ounces) hot-smoked salmon, skinned, flaked coarsely

1 tablespoon thinly sliced lemon rind (see top tips)

METHOD

1 Combine quinoa and the water in a large saucepan; bring to the boil. Reduce heat to low; cook, covered, for 15 minutes or until liquid is absorbed and quinoa is tender. Rinse, drain well.

2 Place snow peas in a heatproof bowl. Cover with boiling water; stand for 2 minutes. Refresh under cold running water; drain well.

3 Place quinoa and snow peas in a large bowl with cucumber and mint; toss to combine. Season to taste. Add combined juice and oil; toss to coat. Serve salad topped with salmon and rind.

TOP TIPS •·······································

Use a zesting tool for the lemon rind. You can use freshly cooked salmon, coarsely flaked smoked trout or smoked chicken as an alternative. Add asparagus and snow pea sprouts for extra crunch.

INFO			SERVES 4	
PREP + COOK TIME 25 MINUTES				
HEALTH FACTOR	GLUTEN FREE	DAIRY FREE	NUT FREE	EGG FREE
FAT	ENERGY	CARB	PROTEIN	FIBRE
16.2g (2.6g sat)	1556kJ (372 cal)	35g	19.3g	5.1g

PER SERVING

CHEESY POLENTA FINGERS

INGREDIENTS

2½ cups (625ml) chicken stock

1 cup (170g) polenta

½ cup (40g) finely grated parmesan

¼ cup (25g) pizza cheese

1 tablespoon olive oil

METHOD

1 Grease a deep 19cm (8-inch) square cake pan; line base and sides with baking paper.

2 Boil stock in a medium saucepan; gradually stir in polenta. Simmer, stirring, for 10 minutes or until thickened. Stir in cheeses. Spread mixture into pan; smooth surface with the back of a spoon. Cover; refrigerate 1 hour or until firm.

3 Turn polenta onto a clean surface; cut into 16 fingers, about 1.5cm x 9.5cm (¾-inch x 4-inch) in size.

4 Brush polenta with oil; cook on a heated oiled grill pan (or grill or barbecue) for 3 minutes each side or until browned lightly and heated through.

TOP TIPS

Polenta can be prepared 2 days ahead; store, covered, in the fridge. The fingers can be eaten cold or warm, and are great in lunchboxes for a healthy snack. Fresh chopped herbs can be stirred through the polenta, if you like.

INFO				SERVES 8

PREP + COOK TIME 25 MINUTES (+ REFRIGERATION)				

HEALTH FACTOR	GLUTEN FREE	EGG FREE	NUT FREE	

FAT	ENERGY	CARB	PROTEIN	FIBRE
2.7g (1g sat)	148kJ (35 cal)	7.6g	2.5g	0.3g

PER SERVING

COCONUT CHICKEN & RICE NOODLE SALAD

This healthy and versatile Asian-style salad makes the perfect office lunch, or packed, it can be enjoyed on a picnic during the summer months.

INGREDIENTS

2 chicken breast fillets (400g)

4 fresh kaffir lime leaves

400ml canned coconut milk

200g (6½ ounces) dried rice stick noodles

½ small wombok (napa cabbage) (350g), shredded finely

1 large carrot (180g), cut into matchsticks

1 cup (80g) bean sprouts

½ cup loosely packed fresh mint leaves

½ cup loosely packed fresh coriander (cilantro) leaves

¼ cup (60ml) lime juice

2 tablespoons brown sugar

2 tablespoons gluten-free fish sauce

METHOD

1 Place chicken and 2 of the lime leaves in a medium saucepan. Add coconut milk and enough cold water to cover the chicken. Bring to a simmer over high heat, then reduce heat to low; simmer, uncovered, for 10 minutes or until chicken is cooked through. Cool completely in cooking liquid.

2 Remove chicken from pan; reserve ¼ cup of the cooking liquid (discard remainder). Coarsely shred the chicken meat into a large bowl; add reserved cooking liquid. Cover with plastic wrap; refrigerate until cold.

3 Place dried noodles in a large heatproof bowl; cover with boiling water. Stand until just tender; drain. Rinse under cold water; drain well.

4 Add noodles, wombok, carrot and sprouts to chicken mixture; toss to combine. Finely shred remaining lime leaves; add to noodle mixture with mint and coriander.

5 Place juice, sugar and sauce in a screw-top jar; shake well. Pour dressing over salad; toss gently to combine. Serve salad with lime wedges, if you like.

• TOP TIPS

Use any style of rice noodle you like. The recipe can be made a day ahead; store, covered, in the fridge. Keep the dressing separate and dress just before serving.

INFO				SERVES 4
PREP + COOK TIME 30 MINUTES (+ COOLING & REFRIGERATION)				
HEALTH FACTOR	GLUTEN FREE	DAIRY FREE	NUT FREE	EGG FREE
FAT	ENERGY	CARB	PROTEIN	FIBRE
4.2g (2.4g sat)	1009kJ (241 cal)	20g	27.7g	5.3g
				PER SERVING

MUSHROOM & TOMATO TARTS

You will need an 8cm (3¼-inch) round cutter.

INGREDIENTS

½ quantity gluten-free pastry (see page 56)

1 teaspoon butter

120g (4 ounces) swiss brown mushrooms, sliced thinly

1 tablespoon red wine vinegar

12 cherry tomatoes, quartered

60g (2 ounces) fetta, crumbled

1 tablespoon fresh oregano leaves

METHOD

1 Grease 12 x 6cm (2½-inch) loose-based fluted tart tins. Roll pastry between sheets of baking paper until 3mm (⅛-inch) thick; cut 12 rounds from pastry using a cutter. Ease pastry into tins, pressing into base and side; trim edges, prick bases with a fork. Place tart tins on an oven tray; cover, refrigerate for 30 minutes.

2 Preheat oven to 180°C/350°F.

3 Bake pastry cases for 10 minutes or until browned lightly. Cool.

4 Melt butter in a small frying pan over high heat, add mushrooms; cook for 3 minutes or until softened. Add vinegar; cook, stirring, until liquid is reduced. Add tomatoes; cook, stirring, until heated through. Remove from heat; season to taste. Cool 10 minutes.

5 Spoon mushroom mixture into tart cases; sprinkle with fetta and oregano just before serving.

INFO				MAKES 12

PREP + COOK TIME 25 MINUTES (+ REFRIGERATION)				

HEALTH FACTOR	GLUTEN FREE	YEAST FREE	NUT FREE	EGG FREE

FAT	ENERGY	CARB	PROTEIN	FIBRE
7.5g (4g sat)	541kJ (129 cal)	13.1g	1.9g	0.7g

PER TART

OLIVE & BACON PIZZA SCROLLS

INGREDIENTS

½ quantity gluten-free pastry (see page 56)

potato flour, for dusting

1½ tablespoons tomato paste

3 rindless gluten-free bacon slices (195g), chopped coarsely

¼ cup (40g) sliced black olives

1 tablespoon coarsely chopped fresh oregano

1 cup (100g) grated mozzarella

METHOD

1 Preheat oven to 220°C/425°F. Oil a 19cm x 29cm (8-inch x 11¾-inch) rectangular pan.

2 Turn pizza dough onto a work surface dusted with potato flour. Roll dough into a 25cm x 30cm (10-inch x 12-inch) rectangle.

3 Spread tomato paste over dough, leaving a 1cm (½-inch) border; sprinkle dough with bacon, olives, oregano and ½ cup of the cheese. Firmly roll dough from long side to enclose filling; trim ends.

4 Cut roll into 12 slices; place slices, cut-side up, in a single layer, in pan.

5 Bake scrolls for 20 minutes; top with remaining cheese. Bake a further 15 minutes or until cheese has melted and turns golden brown. Sprinkle with oregano leaves to serve, if you like.

TOP TIPS •

Serve scrolls warm or cold. This is a great recipe for kids' lunchboxes. You can leave out the olives and oregano if your child doesn't like those flavours, and just make them using bacon and cheese. Store scrolls in an airtight container for 1 day, or freeze, wrapped in plastic wrap, for up to 3 months. To reheat: discard plastic, and wrap frozen scrolls in foil; place in a moderate oven for 30 minutes or until heated through.

INFO			MAKES 12	
PREP + COOK TIME 50 MINUTES				
HEALTH FACTOR	GLUTEN FREE	NUT FREE		
FAT	ENERGY	CARB	PROTEIN	FIBRE
9.6g (2.8g sat)	801kJ (241 cal)	19.4g	6.5g	0.5g

PER SCROLL

TOP TIPS •··

Rice balls can be made 3 days ahead; store, covered, in the refrigerator. The tomato chutney can be made 1 week ahead; store in a sterilised jar (see page 118).

CHEESY RICE BALLS

A twist on an Italian classic, these easy to make balls also make a great appetiser for dinner parties or addition to a salad for a delicious main meal.

INGREDIENTS

$2/3$ cup (130g) white short-grain rice

$1\frac{1}{3}$ cups (330ml) water

150g ($4\frac{1}{2}$ ounces) mozzarella

3 eggs

$\frac{1}{2}$ cup (40g) finely grated parmesan

100g (3 ounces) fetta, crumbled

$2/3$ cup (100g) 100% corn (maize) cornflour (cornstarch)

3 cups (300g) gluten-free breadcrumbs

vegetable oil, for deep-frying

TOMATO CHUTNEY

2 large tomatoes (440g), chopped coarsely

1 medium red onion (170g), chopped coarsely

$1\frac{1}{2}$ tablespoons red wine vinegar

2 cloves garlic, chopped coarsely

1 tablespoon brown sugar

METHOD

1 Combine rice and the water in a medium heavy-based saucepan. Cover tightly, bring to the boil; reduce heat to as low as possible, cook for 10 minutes. Remove pan from heat; stand, covered, for 5 minutes. Fluff rice with a fork; cool.

2 Cut mozzarella into 28 x 5mm ($\frac{1}{4}$-inch) cubes.

3 Combine rice, 1 egg, parmesan and fetta in a medium bowl. Roll rounded tablespoons of rice mixture into 28 balls; press a piece of mozzarella into the centre of each ball, roll to enclose.

4 Lightly beat remaining eggs. Coat balls in cornflour; dip in egg, then coat in breadcrumbs. Place balls on tray, cover; refrigerate for 30 minutes.

5 Meanwhile, make tomato chutney.

6 Heat oil in a large heavy-based saucepan over medium-high heat until oil reaches 190°C/375°F on a sugar thermometer (or when a cube of bread turns golden in about 10 seconds). Deep-fry balls, in batches, for 4 minutes or until golden and heated through; drain on paper towel.

7 Serve rice balls warm or cold with tomato chutney; sprinkle with fresh parsley leaves, if you like.

TOMATO CHUTNEY Place ingredients in a medium saucepan over medium-high heat; cook, uncovered, stirring occasionally, for 10 minutes or until mixture is soft. Blend or process mixture until just combined. Season to taste.

INFO		SERVES 4

PREP + COOK TIME 50 MINUTES (+ REFRIGERATION)		

HEALTH FACTOR	GLUTEN FREE	NUT FREE

FAT	ENERGY	CARB	PROTEIN	FIBRE
37.2g (14.5g sat)	3325kJ (794 cal)	104.8g	30.8g	2.7g

PER SERVING

4 WAYS WITH LUNCHBOX ROLLS

PASTRAMI WITH SILVER BEET COLESLAW

Combine 2 medium finely shredded silver beet (swiss chard) leaves, 1 medium carrot, cut into matchsticks, 1 thinly sliced green onion (scallion), 2 tablespoons plain soy yoghurt and 1½ teaspoons dijon mustard in a medium bowl. Season to taste. Sandwich 100g (3oz) pastrami slices and silver beet mixture between four slices of gluten-free bread.

TUNA WITH QUINOA TABBOULEH

Bring ¼ cup rinsed, drained white quinoa and ¾ cup of water to the boil in a small saucepan over high heat. Reduce heat to low; cook, covered, for 15 minutes or until liquid is absorbed. Cool. Transfer quinoa to a small bowl; add 1 finely chopped medium tomato, 1 finely sliced green onion (scallion), 2 tablespoons each of coarsely chopped fresh flat-leaf parsley and mint, 1 tablespoon olive oil and 1½ tablespoons lemon juice; toss to combine. Fold 95g (3oz) canned drained flaked tuna in oil through salad. Season to taste. Sandwich salad between two small halved gluten-free turkish bread rolls.

INFO	SERVES 2
PREP + COOK TIME 20 MINUTES	

INFO	SERVES 2
PREP + COOK TIME 25 MINUTES (+ COOLING)	

CHAR-GRILLED VEGETABLES & PUMPKIN DIP ROLLS

Drain a 280g (9oz) jar char-grilled vegetables; pat dry with paper towel, season. Sandwich ⅓ cup gluten-free moroccan pumpkin dip, char-grilled vegetables and 20g (¾oz) baby rocket (arugula) leaves between 2 gluten-free torpedo rolls.

CHICKEN, AVOCADO & VEGETABLE ROLLS

Combine ⅓ cup coarsely chopped fresh coriander (cilantro), 2 tablespoons chopped fresh mint, 2 teaspoons finely grated lemon rind and 1 tablespoon each of lemon juice and grapeseed oil in a small bowl; season. Sandwich ½ medium mashed avocado, 1 cup sliced cooked chicken, 1 lebanese cucumber and 1 carrot, both sliced into ribbons, and herb mixture between two halved small gluten-free rolls.

INFO   MAKES 2

PREP + COOK TIME 15 MINUTES

INFO   MAKES 2

PREP + COOK TIME 20 MINUTES

SPICED LENTIL & ROASTED KUMARA SOUP

This wonderfully warming soup combines rich aromatic spices with low-GI ingredients and high-protein for an energy-boosting meal option.

INGREDIENTS

1 large kumara (orange sweet potato) (500g), cut into 2cm (¾-inch) cubes

cooking-oil spray

1 medium brown onion (150g), chopped coarsely

1 clove garlic, crushed

1 cup (250ml) gluten-free vegetable stock

1 teaspoon ground cumin

1 teaspoon ground coriander

½ teaspoon ground turmeric

½ cup (100g) dried red lentils, rinsed, drained

1 litre (4 cups) water

⅔ cup (190g) low-fat gluten-free plain yoghurt

¼ cup finely chopped fresh coriander (cilantro)

METHOD

1 Preheat oven to 220°C/425°F. Place kumara on a baking-paper-lined oven tray; spray with oil. Bake for 25 minutes or until golden and tender.

2 Meanwhile, cook onion, garlic and 2 tablespoons of the stock in a medium saucepan over high heat, stirring, for 3 minutes or until onion is tender. Add spices; cook, stirring, for 30 seconds or until fragrant. Stir in lentils, remaining stock and the water; bring to the boil. Reduce heat; simmer, uncovered, for 15 minutes or until lentils are tender.

3 Add kumara to soup in pan; cook 5 minutes. Remove from heat; cool for 10 minutes.

4 Blend or process mixture, in batches, until smooth. Return mixture to pan; stir over heat until hot. Season to taste.

5 Combine yoghurt and coriander in a small bowl. Serve soup topped with yoghurt mixture and extra coriander leaves.

INFO   SERVES 4

PREP + COOK TIME 45 MINUTES			

HEALTH FACTOR	GLUTEN FREE	EGG FREE	NUT FREE

FAT	ENERGY	CARB	PROTEIN	FIBRE
2.7g (0.5g sat)	877kJ (209 cal)	30.9g	12g	6.7g

PER SERVING

TOP TIPS

Soup can be made a day ahead; store, covered, in the fridge. Freeze the soup without the yoghurt mixture in an airtight container for up to 3 months. Defrost in the fridge overnight then reheat in a small saucepan on the stove over medium heat for about 10 minutes or until hot.

BEETROOT HUMMUS & BEEF WRAP

INGREDIENTS

4 baby beetroot (beets) (100g), unpeeled, trimmed

1 small zucchini (90g), sliced thinly lengthways

420g (13½ ounces) canned chickpeas (garbanzo beans), drained, rinsed

1 tablespoon tahini

1 clove garlic, crushed

1 tablespoon lemon juice

⅓ cup (80ml) olive oil

4 gluten-free wraps (260g)

320g (10 ounces) rare roast beef

80g (2½ ounces) baby rocket (arugula) leaves

METHOD

1 Preheat oven to 180°C/350°F.

2 Wrap each beetroot in a piece of foil; place in a small shallow baking dish. Roast for 50 minutes or until tender. When cool enough to handle, peel beetroot then cut into quarters.

3 Meanwhile, cook zucchini on a heated oiled grill pan (or grill or barbecue) for 3 minutes each side or until tender.

4 Blend or process beetroot, chickpeas, tahini, garlic and juice until combined. With motor operating, gradually add oil in a thin, steady stream; process until mixture is smooth. Season to taste.

5 Spread wraps with beetroot hummus; top with beef, rocket and zucchini, roll to enclose filling.

INFO					MAKES 4
PREP + COOK TIME 1¼ HOURS					
HEALTH FACTOR	GLUTEN FREE	DAIRY FREE	NUT FREE	EGG FREE	YEAST FREE

FAT	ENERGY	CARB	PROTEIN	FIBRE
29g (4.8g sat)	2486kJ (549 cal)	56.9g	23.7g	5.5g

PER WRAP

QUINOA SALAD WITH VEGETABLES

INGREDIENTS

1 medium red capsicum
(bell pepper) (200g), quartered

2 medium zucchini (240g), sliced thinly

2 baby eggplant (120g), sliced thinly

1 medium red onion (170g),
cut into wedges

$\frac{2}{3}$ cup (140g) white quinoa,
rinsed, drained

$1\frac{1}{3}$ cups (320ml) water

1 tablespoon olive oil

$\frac{1}{3}$ cup (80ml) lemon juice

2 teaspoons dijon mustard

425g ($3\frac{1}{2}$ ounces) canned tuna
in springwater, drained

$\frac{1}{3}$ cup loosely packed fresh baby
basil leaves

METHOD

1 Cook capsicum, zucchini, eggplant and onion on a heated oiled grill plate (or grill or barbecue) until tender. Cut capsicum into slices.

2 Meanwhile, place quinoa in a small saucepan with the water; bring to the boil. Reduce heat to low; simmer, covered, for 15 minutes or until tender and water is absorbed. Remove from heat; stand for 10 minutes, then fluff with a fork.

3 Place oil, juice and mustard in a screw-top jar; shake well.

4 Place vegetables and quinoa in a large bowl with tuna and dressing; toss gently to combine. Season to taste. Serve salad topped with basil.

TOP TIPS

Vegetables can be grilled a day ahead; store, covered, in the fridge. This salad can be served warm or cold; add some rocket (arugula) or spinach leaves, if you like.

INFO				SERVES 4

PREP + COOK TIME 25 MINUTES				

HEALTH FACTOR	GLUTEN FREE	DAIRY FREE	NUT FREE	EGG FREE

FAT	ENERGY	CARB	PROTEIN	FIBRE
9.5g (1.9g sat)	1416kJ (338 cal)	29g	30.6g	5.7g

PER SERVING

TOP TIPS •

This recipe is perfect for any lunchbox as you can make it the night before; store, covered, in the fridge. If you are short on time, try making this salad with quinoa instead of rice; it will take less than half the time to cook and has a great fibre content, just like brown rice. You could use chicken breast or lamb fillets instead of the turkey.

TURKEY & BROWN RICE SALAD

Turkey has more protein and less fat that other white meats, while brown rice has a host of health benefits making this a power-packed meal option.

INGREDIENTS

1⅓ cups (200g) brown rice

200g (6½ ounces) green beans, trimmed, halved lengthways

400g (12½ ounces) turkey breast steaks

6 red radishes (210g), sliced thinly

1 lebanese cucumber (130g), halved, sliced thinly

2 green onions (scallions), sliced thinly

2 celery stalks (300g), trimmed, sliced thinly

80g (2½ ounces) goat's cheese, crumbled

2 tablespoons cashews, toasted, chopped coarsely

100g (3 ounces) baby rocket (arugula) leaves

½ cup loosely packed torn fresh basil leaves

2 tablespoons olive oil

⅓ cup (80ml) lemon juice

METHOD

1 Place rice in a medium saucepan, cover with water; bring to the boil. Reduce heat; simmer, uncovered, for 35 minutes or until tender. Drain; rinse under cold water. Drain well.

2 Meanwhile, cook beans in a small saucepan of boiling water for 3 minutes or until just tender. Drain; refresh under cold water, drain.

3 Cook turkey on a heated oiled grill pan (or grill or barbecue) for 3 minutes each side or until cooked through. Cover; rest for 5 minutes, then slice thickly.

4 Combine rice, beans, turkey, radish, cucumber, onion, celery, goat's cheese, nuts, rocket and basil in a large bowl. Drizzle with combined oil and juice; toss to combine. Season to taste.

INFO			SERVES 4	
PREP + COOK TIME 25 MINUTES				
HEALTH FACTOR	GLUTEN FREE	EGG FREE		
FAT 21.2g (5.9g)	ENERGY 2150kJ (513 cal)	CARB 44.5g	PROTEIN 32.7g	FIBRE 5.6g

PER SERVING

HOT & SOUR PRAWN & CHICKEN SOUP

INGREDIENTS

1.5 litres (6 cups) water

4 fresh kaffir lime leaves, torn

80g (2½ ounces) fresh ginger, sliced thickly

1 fresh small red thai (serrano) chilli, sliced thinly

200g (6½ ounces) dried rice noodles

8 green king prawns (shrimp) (280g)

200g (6½ ounces) chicken breast, sliced thinly

2 tablespoons lime juice

200g (6½ ounces) snow peas, shredded

500g (1 pound) baby choy sum, trimmed, chopped

1 cup (80g) bean sprouts

½ cup loosely packed fresh coriander (cilantro) leaves

½ cup loosely packed fresh mint leaves

½ cup loosely packed fresh thai basil leaves

METHOD

1 Combine the water, lime leaves, ginger and half the chilli in a medium saucepan over high heat; bring to the boil. Reduce heat; simmer, covered, for 10 minutes. Discard leaves and ginger.

2 Meanwhile, cook noodles in a medium saucepan of boiling water according to packet directions; drain.

3 Shell and devein prawns, leaving tails intact. Add prawns and chicken to broth; simmer for 5 minutes or until chicken and prawns are cooked. Stir in juice.

4 Divide noodles, snow peas and choy sum among four serving bowls; ladle over broth mixture. Top with sprouts, herbs and remaining chilli.

INFO				SERVES 4
PREP + COOK TIME 30 MINUTES				
HEALTH FACTOR	GLUTEN FREE	DAIRY FREE	NUT FREE	EGG FREE
FAT 3.8g (0.9g sat)	ENERGY 1101kJ (263 cal)	CARB 28.4g	PROTEIN 25g	FIBRE 5.8g

PER SERVING

GLUTEN-FREE BREAD

INGREDIENTS

3 cups (405g) gluten-free plain (all-purpose) flour

½ cup (75g) potato flour

½ cup (80g) brown rice flour

½ cup (80g) white rice flour

3 teaspoons (10g) dried yeast

2 teaspoons salt

2 teaspoons xantham gum

1 egg

3 egg whites

¾ cup (180ml) olive oil

1 teaspoon vinegar

2 cups (500ml) warm water

1 tablespoon olive oil, extra

2 teaspoons salt, extra

METHOD

1 Grease a 12cm x 20cm (4¾-inch x 8-inch) loaf pan; lightly dust with rice flour.

2 Combine sifted flours, yeast, salt and gum in a large bowl.

3 Place egg, egg whites, oil, vinegar and 1½ cups of the water in a large bowl of an electric mixer; beat on medium speed for 3½ minutes. Add remaining water and the flour mixture, 1 cup at a time, beating until combined and smooth.

4 Spoon mixture into loaf pan; smooth the surface. Cover; stand in a warm place for 45 minutes.

5 Preheat oven to 220°C/425°F.

6 Drizzle loaf with extra oil and sprinkle with extra salt. Bake for 1 hour or until crust is firm and golden brown and the loaf sounds hollow when tapped. Stand bread in pan for 5 minutes before turning, top-side up, onto a wire rack to cool.

INFO	MAKES 1 LOAF (12 SLICES)			
PREP + COOK TIME 1½ HOURS (+ STANDING)				
HEALTH FACTOR	GLUTEN FREE	DAIRY FREE	NUT FREE	
FAT	ENERGY	CARB	PROTEIN	FIBRE
16.1g (2.4g sat)	1400kJ (335 cal)	43.8g	3g	0.7g
				PER SLICE

TOP TIPS

This bread is best eaten the day it is baked, however, it's great for toast or toasted sandwiches the next day. This mixture will make 6 gluten-free bread rolls – divide dough into 6 even portions, roll into balls and place on a greased and floured oven tray, stand 45 minutes. Drizzle rolls with oil and sprinkle with salt; bake for 30 minutes.

CHERMOULLA TUNA, CHICKPEA & BROAD BEAN SALAD

Chermoulla is an exotic blend of fragrant spices traditionally used in Moroccan cooking to add a 'kick' to seafood, meat and poultry.

INGREDIENTS

400g (12½-ounce) piece tuna steak

2 cup (300g) frozen broad (fava) beans

200g (6½ ounces) green beans, trimmed, cut into thirds

840g (1¾ pounds) canned chickpeas (garbanzo beans), drained, rinsed

1 cup firmly packed fresh flat-leaf parsley leaves

2 medium lemons (280g), segmented (see top tips)

2 tablespoons lemon juice

2 tablespoons olive oil

CHERMOULLA

1 small red onion (100g), chopped coarsely

1 clove garlic, peeled

2 cups firmly packed fresh coriander (cilantro) leaves, chopped coarsely

2 cups firmly packed fresh flat-leaf parsley leaves, chopped coarsely

2 teaspoons ground cumin

2 teaspoons smoked paprika

2 tablespoons olive oil

METHOD

1 Make chermoulla; reserve three-quarters to serve.

2 Place tuna in a shallow dish with remaining chermoulla; toss to coat. Cover; refrigerate 30 minutes.

3 Meanwhile, place broad beans in a heatproof bowl, cover with boiling water; stand for 2 minutes. Rinse under cold water; drain. Peel beans.

4 Boil, steam or microwave green beans until just tender; drain, rinse under cold water, drain.

5 Cook tuna on a heated oiled grill plate (or grill or barbecue) for 2 minutes each side or until slightly charred on the outside but still rare in the centre. Cover; stand for 5 minutes. Slice tuna, across the grain.

6 Combine broad beans, green beans, chickpeas, parsley and lemon segments in a medium bowl with combined juice and oil. Serve tuna with salad and top with reserved chermoulla.

CHERMOULLA Blend or process ingredients until just combined. Season to taste.

INFO				SERVES 4
PREP + COOK TIME 30 MINUTES (+ REFRIGERATION)				

HEALTH FACTOR	GLUTEN FREE	DAIRY FREE	NUT FREE	EGG FREE

FAT	ENERGY	CARB	PROTEIN	FIBRE
23.6g (3.7g)	2208kJ (527 cal)	29.6g	43.7g	18.1g

PER SERVING

TOP TIPS

To segment the lemons, cut off the rind with the white pith, following the curve of the fruit. Cut down either side of each segment close to the membrane to release the segment. Purchase sashimi grade tuna for this recipe. Swap the tuna for salmon if you like. If the chermoulla ingredients aren't blending well, add 1 tablespoon water to the mixture.

VIETNAMESE PANCAKES WITH PRAWNS

This traditional dish is eaten by tearing off a piece of pancake and placing it inside a lettuce leaf, with prawns, sprouts and herbs, then rolling it up.

INGREDIENTS

16 cooked tiger prawns (shrimp) (560g)

1 cup (180g) rice flour

½ teaspoon ground turmeric

⅓ cup (80ml) reduced-fat coconut milk

1⅓ cups (330ml) water

2 eggs

2 tablespoons olive oil

16 butter (boston) lettuce leaves
   (from the centre of the lettuce)

2 lebanese cucumber (260g),
   sliced into ribbons

2 medium carrots (240g),
   sliced into ribbons

2 cups (160g) bean sprouts

1 bunch fresh mint leaves

1 bunch fresh thai basil leaves

CHILLI DIPPING SAUCE

2 tablespoons warm water

2 tablespoons lemon juice

1 tablespoon caster (superfine) sugar

1 teaspoon gluten-free fish sauce

1 clove garlic, crushed

1 fresh small red thai (serrano) chilli,
   chopped finely

METHOD

1 Make chilli dipping sauce.

2 Shell and devein prawns, leaving tails intact.

3 Place rice flour and turmeric in a medium bowl. Whisk in coconut milk, the water and eggs until well combined and batter is smooth.

4 Heat 1 teaspoon of the oil in a large non-stick frying pan (base measurement 23cm/9 inches) over medium heat; pour a quarter of the batter into pan, swirl around base to form a thin pancake. Cook for 2 minutes or until batter has set. Slide pancake onto a serving plate. Repeat to make eight pancakes in total.

5 Serve pancakes with lettuce, prawns, cucumber, carrot, sprouts, herbs and chilli dipping sauce.

CHILLI DIPPING SAUCE Stir the water, juice and sugar in a small bowl until sugar has dissolved. Add remaining ingredients; stir to combine.

INFO				SERVES 4
PREP + COOK TIME 30 MINUTES				

HEALTH FACTOR	GLUTEN FREE	DAIRY FREE	NUT FREE

FAT	ENERGY	CARB	PROTEIN	FIBRE
14.7g (3.9g)	1800kJ (430 cal)	47.1g	23.5g	6.5g

PER SERVING

TOP TIPS
Use a vegetable peeler to slice thin ribbons from the cucumber and carrot.

DINNER

For many families, dinner time is the most
important meal of the day, providing a chance
for the whole household to sit together and
talk about their day. Whether it is a quick and
easy meal to cook during the week, a lavish
weekend affair or a tasty gluten-free twist
on some family favourites, the recipes in
this section will inspire and excite.

PEANUT-FREE SATAY CHICKEN SKEWERS

This tasty alternative to traditional satay sauce uses nut-free butter made from roasted sunflower seeds, and is also dairy and egg-free.

INGREDIENTS

⅓ cup (95g) nut-free butter

270ml canned coconut milk

2 tablespoons gluten-free tamari

2 tablespoons sweet chilli sauce

2 tablespoons lime juice

2 tablespoons gluten-free tamari, extra

1 teaspoon sweet chilli sauce, extra

12 chicken tenderloins (640g)

200g (6½ ounces) snow peas, trimmed, sliced

2 cups (300g) cooked jasmine rice

2 tablespoons fresh coriander (cilantro) leaves

METHOD

1 Heat a small heavy-based saucepan over medium heat; cook nut-free butter and coconut milk, without boiling, stirring until smooth. Stir in tamari, sweet chilli sauce and juice; cook, stirring for 1 minute or until hot.

2 Combine extra tamari and extra sweet chilli sauce in a small bowl. Thread chicken onto 12 skewers; season. Cook chicken on a heated, oiled grill pan (or barbecue or grill) for about 2 minutes each side or until cooked through; brush with half the tamari mixture in the final minute of cooking.

3 Meanwhile, boil, steam or microwave snow peas until just tender. Combine snow peas with remaining tamari mixture until coated.

4 Serve chicken on rice with snow peas and satay sauce; sprinkle with coriander.

SERVING SUGGESTION Serve with stir-fried asian greens.

TOP TIPS

Nut-free butter is available in smooth and crunchy varieties, from health food stores, some larger supermarkets and online. You need to cook ⅔ cup jasmine rice for the amount of cooked rice needed.

INFO				SERVES 4
PREP + COOK TIME 30 MINUTES				
HEALTH FACTOR	GLUTEN FREE	DAIRY FREE	NUT FREE	EGG FREE
FAT 35g (16.5g sat)	ENERGY 2737kJ (654 cal)	CARB 36.8g	PROTEIN 46.1g	FIBRE 2.9g

PER SERVING

GLUTEN-FREE PASTRY

INGREDIENTS

**375g (12-ounce) packet
gluten-free pastry mix**

**125g (4 ounces) cold butter,
chopped coarsely**

⅔ cup (160ml) water

2 tablespoons gluten-free tamari

2 tablespoons olive oil

**gluten-free plain (all-purpose) flour,
for dusting**

METHOD

1 Place pastry mix in a large bowl; rub
in butter until mixture resembles coarse
breadcrumbs. Add enough of the combined
water, tamari and oil until mixture comes
together. Lightly knead on a surface dusted
with a little gluten-free flour into a ball.

2 Roll pastry between two sheets of
baking paper until 5mm (¼-inch)
thick. Pastry is now ready to use.

TOP TIPS ●··································

Pastry is best used straight away. Rolling the pastry
between sheets of baking paper will prevent the dough
from sticking to the bench. If pastry dries out while you
are using it, add a little olive oil to the dough. If pastry
cracks when you are rolling it out or placing it into tart
cases etc, it can quickly and easily be pushed back
together without ruining it.

INFO	MAKES 640g SHORTCRUST PASTRY			
PREP + COOK TIME 10 MINUTES				
HEALTH FACTOR	GLUTEN FREE	DAIRY FREE	NUT FREE	YEAST FREE
FAT 142.6g (73g sat)	ENERGY 10744kJ (2567 cal)	CARB 30.2g	PROTEIN 13.3g	FIBRE 7.5g

PER QUANTITY

SAUSAGE ROLLS

INGREDIENTS

2 teaspoons olive oil

1 small leek (200g), chopped finely

1 small carrot (70g), grated finely

1 clove garlic, crushed

300g (9½ ounces) sausage mince

½ teaspoon roast lamb seasoning

1 tablespoon tomato paste

1½ rolls (600g) packaged gluten-free shortcrust pastry (see top tips)

gluten-free plain (all-purpose) flour, for dusting

3 teaspoons sesame seeds or poppy seeds

METHOD

1 Heat oil in a medium frying pan over high heat; cook leek, carrot and garlic, stirring, for 5 minutes or until soft. Cool.

2 Combine mince, seasoning, paste and vegetable mixture in a medium bowl; season.

3 Roll pastry on a surface dusted with gluten-free flour until 4mm (¼ inch) thick; cut into six 12cm (6½-inch) squares. Spoon ⅓ cups of mixture down one edge of each square. Roll to enclose. Brush edges with a little water; press to seal. Score pastry with a sharp knife; sprinkle with seeds. Refrigerate for 30 minutes or until firm.

4 Preheat oven to 180°C/350°F. Oil a baking tray; line with baking paper. Place rolls on tray.

5 Bake rolls for 20 minutes or until pastry is browned lightly and filling is cooked through. Serve with mustard or gluten-free tomato sauce (ketchup).

INFO				MAKES 6
PREP + COOK TIME 1 HOUR (+ REFRIGERATION)				
HEALTH FACTOR	GLUTEN FREE	YEAST FREE	NUT FREE	EGG FREE
FAT 30g (13.7g sat)	ENERGY 2087kJ (498 cal)	CARB 44.1g	PROTEIN 12.7g	FIBRE 2.4g

PER ROLL

TOP TIPS

Gluten-free shortcrust pastry comes in 400g (12½-ounce) rolls; it is available from most major supermarkets in the freezer section. If using the gluten-free pastry on page 56, you will need one quantity.

CHICKEN SCHNITZEL WITH CORN TOMATO SALAD

This family favourite is given a superfood makeover with a healthy quinoa coating blended with delicious herbs and spices for extra taste.

INGREDIENTS

2 medium red capsicums (bell peppers) (400g), chopped coarsely

200g (6½ ounces) red grape tomatoes

1½ tablespoons olive oil

2 trimmed corn cobs (500g)

4 chicken breast fillets (800g)

½ cup (125ml) soy milk

2 teaspoons smoked paprika

1 cup (100g) quinoa flakes

1 tablespoon finely chopped fresh lemon thyme

vegetable oil, for shallow-frying

1 tablespoon red wine vinegar

1 teaspoon dijon mustard

2 green onions (scallions), sliced thinly

½ cup loosely packed fresh coriander (cilantro) leaves

METHOD

1 Preheat oven to 160°C/325°F.

2 Place capsicum and tomatoes in a roasting pan; drizzle with 2 teaspoons of the olive oil. Roast for 20 minutes or until tomatoes begin to soften.

3 Meanwhile, cook corn on a heated oiled grill plate (or grill or barbecue), turning occasionally, for 15 minutes or until corn is lightly charred and tender. Cool slightly. When cool enough to handle, cut down the cobs with a sharp knife to remove the kernels. Place in a large bowl.

4 Using a sharp knife, cut each chicken breast in half widthways. Place a chicken half between two pieces of plastic wrap; gently pound with a meat mallet or rolling pin until 1cm (½-inch) thick. Repeat with remaining chicken halves.

5 Combine soy milk and 1 teaspoon of paprika in a large bowl, season; add chicken, toss to coat.

6 Combine quinoa, thyme and remaining paprika in a large shallow bowl. Remove chicken, one piece at a time, from milk mixture; gently shake off excess, dip into quinoa mixture to coat.

7 Heat enough vegetable oil in a large frying pan to come 2cm (¾-inch) up the side of the pan, over medium-high heat; cook chicken, in batches, for 2 minutes each side or until chicken is golden brown and cooked through. Drain on paper towel.

8 Place vinegar, mustard and remaining olive oil in a screw-top jar; shake well, season to taste.

9 Add capsicum mixture to corn with green onion, coriander and dressing; toss gently to combine. Serve chicken with salad.

INFO					SERVES 4
PREP + COOK TIME 1 HOUR					
HEALTH FACTOR	GLUTEN FREE	DAIRY FREE	NUT FREE	YEAST FREE	EGG FREE

FAT	ENERGY	CARB	PROTEIN	FIBRE
40.2g (7.5g sat)	3135kJ (749 cal)	40.1g	53.6g	7.3g

PER SERVING

SMOKED TROUT, PEA & ASPARAGUS RISOTTO

INGREDIENTS

1 litre (4 cups) gluten-free vegetable stock

2 cups (500ml) water

1 tablespoon olive oil

1 medium brown onion (150g), chopped finely

1½ cups (300g) arborio rice

170g (5½ ounces) asparagus, trimmed, cut into 4cm (1½-inch) pieces

100g (3 ounces) snow peas, sliced thinly lengthways

½ cup (60g) fresh or frozen peas

2 teaspoons finely grated lemon rind

2 tablespoons lemon juice

2 tablespoons finely chopped fresh chives

1 tablespoon coarsely chopped fresh dill

150g (4½ ounces) hot-smoked trout, flaked coarsely

METHOD

1 Bring stock and the water to the boil in a small saucepan; reduce heat to low, simmer, covered.

2 Meanwhile, heat oil in a large saucepan over medium heat; cook onion, stirring, for 5 minutes or until soft. Add rice; stir to coat in onion mixture. Stir in 1 cup of the simmering stock mixture; cook, stirring, over low heat until liquid is absorbed.

3 Continue adding the simmering stock in ½-cup batches, stirring, until liquid is absorbed after each addition. Total cooking time should be about 20 minutes or until rice is tender.

4 Add asparagus, snow peas and peas to pan; cook, stirring, for 1 minute or until just tender. Remove from heat. Stir in rind, juice and herbs until just combined. Gently fold through trout, season. Serve topped with a little extra dill and lemon rind.

INFO				SERVES 4
PREF + COOK TIME 45 MINUTES				
HEALTH FACTOR	GLUTEN FREE	DAIRY FREE	NUT FREE	EGG FREE
FAT	ENERGY	CARB	PROTEIN	FIBRE
4.6g (1g sat)	1631kJ (389 cal)	65.8g	18.8g	3.2g

PER SERVING

TOP TIPS

Use a zesting tool to make the thin strips of lemon rind. Add mint instead of chives or dill for a different flavour. Trout can be swapped for hot-smoked salmon. The risotto is best made just before serving.

BACON, CHIVE & POTATO QUICHE

INGREDIENTS

20g (¾ ounce) butter, melted

1 large potato (300g), chopped coarsely

4 rindless gluten-free bacon slices (260g), chopped coarsely

1 quantity gluten-free pastry (see page 56)

½ cup (60g) coarsely grated tasty cheddar

5 eggs, beaten lightly

½ cup (125ml) milk

2 tablespoons finely chopped fresh chives

METHOD

1 Preheat oven to 220°C/425°F. Grease a 24cm (9½-inch) round loose-based fluted flan tin with the melted butter.

2 Boil, steam or microwave potato until tender; drain.

3 Cook bacon in a medium frying pan over high heat, stirring, for 5 minutes or until golden. Remove from pan; drain on paper towel.

4 Roll pastry between two sheets of baking paper until 5mm (¼ inch) thick. Ease pastry into pan, pushing together any cracks that might form. Press pastry into side and base of pan; trim edges.

TOP TIPS You can make this into six individual quiches. Use store-bought gluten-free shortcrust pastry, available from major supermarkets, if you like.

5 Sprinkle bacon, potato and cheddar into pastry case. Whisk eggs, milk and chives in a medium jug, season; pour over bacon mixture.

6 Bake quiche for 30 minutes or until set.

SERVING SUGGESTION Serve with a mixed green salad.

INFO				SERVES 6
PREP + COOK TIME 1 HOUR				
HEALTH FACTOR	GLUTEN FREE	DAIRY FREE	NUT FREE	

FAT	ENERGY	CARB	PROTEIN	FIBRE
40.9g (20.3g sat)	2874kJ (687 cal)	57.8g	20.6g	2.1g

PER SERVING

BEEF PIES

The first pies were made by the Romans, the crust was used as a way to cook the meat then was discarded. These pies are also dairy and egg-free.

INGREDIENTS

1 tablespoon olive oil

800g (1½ pounds) gravy beef, cut into 2cm (¾-inch) pieces

2 medium brown onions (300g), chopped finely

1 clove garlic, crushed

2 tablespoons tomato paste

1 tablespoon dijon mustard

2½ cups (625ml) gluten-free beef stock

2 tablespoons 100% corn (maize) cornflour (cornstarch)

2 tablespoons water

1 quantity gluten-free pastry (see page 56)

METHOD

1 Heat oil in a medium saucepan over high heat; cook beef, in batches, stirring, for 2 minutes or until browned. Remove from pan.

2 Reduce heat to medium; cook onion and garlic in same pan, stirring, for 5 minutes or until onion is softened. Return beef to pan with combined paste, mustard and beef stock; bring to the boil. Reduce heat to low; simmer, uncovered, stirring, occasionally, for 1½ hours or until beef is tender and sauce thickens.

3 Combine cornflour and the water; add to beef mixture. Cook, stirring, over high heat, for 5 minutes or until sauce boils and thickens. Season to taste. Cool.

4 Preheat oven to 220°C/425°F. Oil six 10cm (4-inch), ¾ cup (180ml) pie dishes. Place dishes on an oven tray.

5 Roll pastry between two sheets of baking paper until 5mm (¼ inch) thick. Cut six 15cm (6-inch) rounds from pastry. Ease pastry rounds into dishes, press into base and sides; trim edges.

6 Spoon beef mixture into pastry cases. Brush edges with water. Cut six 10cm (5¼-inch) rounds from remaining pastry; place on pies, press to seal, trim edges. Refrigerate 30 minutes.

7 Make two small cuts into the top of each pie. Bake for 30 minutes or until tops are firm, browned lightly and filling is hot.

SERVING SUGGESTION Serve with peas and gluten-free oven-baked chips.

INFO   MAKES 6

PREP + COOK TIME 2½ HOURS (+ COOLING & REFRIGERATION)					
HEALTH FACTOR	GLUTEN FREE	DAIRY FREE	NUT FREE	YEAST FREE	EGG FREE

FAT	ENERGY	CARB	PROTEIN	FIBRE
34.3g (14.5g sat)	2673kJ (638 cal)	50.5g	33.7g	2.4g

PER PIE

TOP TIPS

You can use store-bought gluten-free puff pastry, available from major supermarkets. The pies can be cooked in an electric pie maker. Freeze pies for up to 3 months; reheat from frozen in a moderate oven for 30 minutes or until pies are heated through.

FAMILY ROAST CHICKEN & CORN PIE

INGREDIENTS

1 tablespoon olive oil

1 small leek (200g), sliced thinly

500g (1 pound) frozen corn kernels

2 tablespoons 100% corn (maize) cornflour (cornstarch)

2 cups (500ml) gluten-free chicken stock

3 cups (480g) coarsely shredded cooked chicken

2 tablespoons coarsely chopped fresh tarragon

1 quantity gluten-free pastry (see page 56)

2 teaspoons sesame seeds

METHOD

1 Preheat oven to 200°C/400°F.

2 Heat oil in a large frying pan over high heat; cook leek, stirring, for 5 minutes or until softened. Add corn; cook, stirring, for 5 minutes or until hot.

3 Combine cornflour with 2 tablespoons of the stock in a small jug until smooth; stir in remaining stock.

4 Add chicken and stock mixture to corn mixture; cook, stirring occasionally, for 5 minutes or until sauce boils and thickens. Remove from heat. Stir in tarragon; season. Cool slightly.

5 Roll pastry between two sheets of baking paper until 5mm (¼ inch) thick.

6 Spoon chicken mixture into a 2-litre (8-cup) ovenproof dish; top with pastry, trim edges. Brush pastry with a little water, sprinkle with sesame seeds. Make a small cut in the centre of the pastry.

7 Bake pie for 25 minutes or until golden brown and filling is heated through.

INFO				SERVES 6
PREP + COOK TIME 1 HOURS				
HEALTH FACTOR	GLUTEN FREE	YEAST FREE	NUT FREE	EGG FREE
FAT	ENERGY	CARB	PROTEIN	FIBRE
33.5g (14.4g sat)	2778kJ (664 cal)	69.1g	22.1g	4.1g

PER SERVING

• TOP TIPS

We used a barbecued chicken. If preferred, you can use store bought gluten-free puff pastry, available from major supermarkets; you will need 1 sheet for this recipe. If you don't like the aniseed flavour of tarragon, you can replace with coarsely chopped fresh chives or flat-leaf parsley.

GLUTEN-FREE PIZZA DOUGH

INGREDIENTS

3 cups (405g) gluten-free plain (all-purpose) flour

1 cup (135g) gluten-free self-raising flour

½ cup (75g) potato flour

½ cup (80g) brown rice flour

½ cup (90g) white rice flour

2 teaspoons (7g) dried yeast

2 teaspoons xantham gum

2 teaspoons salt

1 egg

3 egg whites

¾ cup (180ml) olive oil

1 teaspoon white vinegar

2 cups (500ml) warm water, approximately

white rice flour, extra, for dusting

METHOD

1 Grease three 30cm (12-inch) round pizza trays, dust lightly with a little rice flour.

2 Combine dry ingredients in a large bowl.

3 Beat egg, egg whites, oil, vinegar and 1½ cups of the water in a large bowl of an electric mixer on medium speed for 3½ minutes. Add the combined sifted dry ingredients, 1 cup at a time, beating until combined between additions. Continue adding dry ingredients until mixture just starts to come away from the side of the bowl (add remaining water if necessary). Turn dough onto a surface dusted with rice flour; knead lightly until smooth.

4 Divide dough into three equal portions. Roll each portion on the rice-floured surface until large enough to fit pizza trays. Lift dough onto trays. Cover; stand in a warm place for 45 minutes.

5 Spread pizza dough with sauces and toppings as desired. (For pizza topping suggestions, see recipes on pages 66 and 67).

INFO			MAKES 3 BASES		
PREP + COOK TIME 30 MINUTES (+ STANDING)					
HEALTH FACTOR	GLUTEN FREE	DAIRY FREE	NUT FREE		
FAT	ENERGY	CARB	PROTEIN	FIBRE	
58.5g (8.6g sat)	6090kJ (1455 cal)	216.3g	12.6g	3g	
				PER SERVING	

• TOP TIPS

Divide the dough into 6 equal portions to make mini pizzas. To freeze pizza bases, par-bake pizza dough for 15 minutes or until browned lightly, then cool. Wrap individually in plastic wrap, then foil. Freeze for up to 3 months.

ROASTED VEGETABLE & BOCCONCINI PIZZA

INGREDIENTS

rice flour, for dusting

⅓ quantity gluten-free pizza dough (see page 65)

200g (6½ ounces) pumpkin, cut into 1cm (½-inch) cubes

1 medium zucchini (120g), sliced thinly

1 small red capsicum (bell pepper) (150g), quartered

1 small eggplant (230g), sliced thinly

¼ cup (65g) tomato pasta sauce

1 cup (100g) pizza cheese

100g (3 ounces) baby bocconcini

40g (1½ ounces) rocket (arugula) leaves

METHOD

1 Preheat oven to 220°C/425°F.

2 Oil a 30cm (12-inch) round pizza tray or oven tray, then dust with rice flour. Roll pizza dough on a surface dusted with rice flour into a 30cm (12-inch) round; place on tray. Cover; stand until needed.

3 Place pumpkin on an oiled baking tray; roast for 20 minutes or until tender and cubes are browned around the edges.

4 Meanwhile, cook zucchini, capsicum and eggplant on a heated oiled grill pan (or grill or barbecue) until browned lightly and tender. Season to taste.

5 Spread pizza base with sauce; top with pizza cheese, vegetables and bocconcini.

6 Bake pizza for 15 minutes or until cheese is golden and base is crisp. Just before serving, top with rocket.

INFO				SERVES 4
PREP + COOK TIME 50 MINUTES				
HEALTH FACTOR	GLUTEN FREE	NUT FREE		

FAT	ENERGY	CARB	PROTEIN	FIBRE
26.1g (9.2g sat)	2372kJ (567 cal)	61.4g	19.2g	4.2g

PER SERVING

TOP TIPS

You can use a store-bought gluten-free pizza base instead. If the pizza base is not crisping as much as you would like, place the cooked pizza on an oiled, heated grill pan (or barbecue plate) for a few minutes.

PUTTENESCA PIZZA

INGREDIENTS

rice flour, for dusting

⅓ quantity gluten-free pizza dough (see page 65)

250g (8 ounces) baby roma (egg) tomatoes

1 teaspoon olive oil

200g (6½ ounces) canned diced tomatoes

4 drained anchovy fillets, chopped finely

1 tablespoon fresh rosemary sprigs

1 cup (100g) pizza cheese

100g (3 ounces) thinly sliced gluten-free danish salami

¼ cup (40g) mixed pitted olives, sliced thinly

¼ teaspoon dried chilli flakes

rosemary sprigs, extra, to serve

oregano leaves, to serve (optional)

METHOD

1 Preheat oven to 220°C/450°F.

2 Oil a 30cm (12-inch) round pizza tray or oven tray, then dust with rice flour. Roll dough on a surface dusted with rice flour into a 30cm (12-inch) round; place on tray. Cover; stand until needed.

3 Place roma tomatoes on a baking tray; drizzle with oil, season. Roast for 10 minutes or until just softened.

4 Meanwhile, place canned tomatoes, anchovy and rosemary in a medium frying pan over high heat; cook, stirring, for 5 minutes or until thickened slightly. Season to taste.

5 Spread pizza base with tomato mixture; top with pizza cheese, roasted tomatoes, salami, olives and chilli flakes.

6 Bake pizza for 20 minutes or until golden brown and cheese melts. Just before serving, top with extra rosemary and oregano.

SERVING SUGGESTION
Serve with a mixed salad of baby rocket (arugula) leaves, semi-dried tomato and shaved parmesan.

INFO				SERVES 4
PREP + COOK TIME 45 MINUTES				
HEALTH FACTOR	GLUTEN FREE	NUT FREE		

FAT	ENERGY	CARB	PROTEIN	FIBRE
31.7g (9.3g sat)	2509kJ (599 cal)	59.5g	17.3g	1.8g

PER SERVING

TANDOORI LAMB CUTLETS WITH GREEN ONION ROTI

Tandoori is a popular Indian dish, named after the traditional clay oven it is prepared in. This dish uses ready-made tandoori paste for convenience.

INGREDIENTS

12 french-trimmed lamb cutlets (600g)

1 tablespoon tandoori paste

2 lebanese cucumbers (260g), sliced into ribbons

400g (12½ ounces) red radishes, sliced thinly

1 tablespoon white vinegar

1 tablespoon caster (superfine) sugar

1 cup loosely packed fresh mint leaves

1 cup loosely packed fresh coriander leaves (cilantro)

GREEN ONION ROTI

1 teaspoon cumin seeds

1 green onion (scallion), sliced thinly

1 cup (150g) chickpea (besan) flour

¼ teaspoon xantham gum

2 tablespoons buttermilk

2 tablespoons water

1 tablespoon vegetable oil

chickpea (besan) flour, extra, for dusting

2 tablespoons ghee, melted

METHOD

1 Combine lamb and tandoori paste in a large bowl. Cover; refrigerate for 30 minutes.

2 Meanwhile, make green onion roti.

3 Place cucumber, radish, vinegar and sugar in a medium bowl; toss until sugar dissolves. Stand for 5 minutes to allow vegetables to pickle; drain. Add herbs; toss to combine.

4 Cook lamb on a heated oiled grill plate (or barbecue or grill) for 2 minutes each side or until cooked as desired. Cover lamb; rest for 5 minutes before serving with cucumber salad and roti.

GREEN ONION ROTI Stir cumin in a small dry frying pan, over medium heat, for 1 minute or until fragrant. Combine cumin, green onion, chickpea flour and xantham gum in a large bowl; season. Add buttermilk, the water and oil; stir to form a firm dough. Divide dough into eight balls. Flour work surface with extra chickpea flour; roll out each ball into 2mm (⅛-inch) thick, 12cm (4¾-inch) rounds. Brush a heated small frying pan with ghee; cook roti, over high heat, for 1 minute each side or until lightly golden and cooked through. Transfer to a plate, cover with foil to keep warm. Repeat with remaining roti dough and ghee.

INFO				SERVES 4
PREP + COOK TIME 40 MINUTES (+ REFRIGERATION)				
HEALTH FACTOR	GLUTEN FREE	YEAST FREE	NUT FREE	EGG FREE
FAT	ENERGY	CARB	PROTEIN	FIBRE
23.9g (9.2g sat)	1865kJ (446 cal)	28.8g	25.2g	8.2g
				PER SERVING

TOP TIPS

Roti can be made a day ahead. To reheat, warm in a heated dry frying pan, or wrap in foil and place in a moderate preheated oven for 10 minutes or until heated through.

POTATO & PUMPKIN GNOCCHI WITH ROCKET PESTO

Impress family and friends with this easy-to-make homemade gnocchi.

INGREDIENTS

3 medium potatoes (600g), unpeeled (see top tips)

800g (1½ pounds) pumpkin, cut into cubes

3 teaspoons olive oil

⅓ cup (25g) finely grated parmesan

⅔ cup (90g) gluten-free plain (all-purpose) flour, approximately

15g (½ ounce) baby rocket (arugula) leaves

ROCKET PESTO

1 cup loosely packed fresh basil leaves

15g (½ ounce) baby rocket (arugula) leaves

½ cup (40g) finely grated parmesan

1 clove garlic, crushed

⅓ cup (80ml) olive oil

METHOD

1 Preheat oven to 180°C/375°F.

2 Prick unpeeled potatoes with a fork. Place on a baking tray; roast for 45 minutes.

3 Place pumpkin on a baking-paper-lined oven tray; drizzle with 1 teaspoon of the oil, season and toss to coat. Roast, alongside potato, for final 30 minutes of potato cooking time, or until potato and pumpkin are tender.

4 Meanwhile, make pesto; season.

5 When cool enough to handle, peel potatoes. Using a ricer, mouli or a fine sieve and a wooden spoon, mash potato and half the pumpkin in a large bowl until smooth; season. Stir in cheese and ½ cup of the flour to make a firm dough. Add remaining flour if needed.

6 Divide dough into 4 equal portions. Roll each portion on a gluten-free-floured surface into 2cm (¾-inch) thick sausage shapes; cut each into 3cm (1¼-inch) pieces, roll into balls. Roll each ball along the tines of a fork, pressing lightly on top of ball with your index finger to form a classic gnocchi shape, with grooves on one side and a dimple on the other.

7 Cook gnocchi, in three batches, in a large saucepan of boiling water, uncovered, for 2 minutes or until gnocchi float to the surface. Continue cooking for 2 minutes. Remove from pan with a slotted spoon; drain.

8 Heat remaining oil in a medium frying pan over high heat; cook gnocchi and remaining pumpkin, in two batches, stirring gently, for 2 minutes or until pumpkin is golden.

9 Return gnocchi and pumpkin to the pan; toss through rocket pesto. Serve gnocchi with baby rocket leaves and, if you like, sprinkle with shaved parmesan.

ROCKET PESTO Process basil, rocket, parmesan and garlic until finely chopped. With motor operating, add oil in a thin, steady stream; process until combined.

INFO				SERVES 4
PREP + COOK TIME 1¼ HOURS				
HEALTH FACTOR	GLUTEN FREE	EGG FREE	NUT FREE	
FAT 27.5g (6.4g sat)	ENERGY 2105kJ (503 cal)	CARB 48.6g	PROTEIN 12.1g	FIBRE 7g
				PER SERVING

TOP TIPS

We used sebago potatoes for this recipe – a dry floury potato, that holds its shape well when boiled. Both the gnocchi and the rocket pesto can be made a day ahead; store separately, covered, in the fridge. Swap the rocket for baby spinach leaves, if you like.

SPICY LAMB, SPINACH & FETTA PIZZAS

INGREDIENTS

rice flour, for dusting

⅓ quantity gluten-free pizza dough
(see page 65)

1 tablespoon olive oil

250g (8 ounces) minced (ground) lamb

½ teaspoon ground cumin

½ teaspoon ground coriander

½ teaspoon ground cinnamon

½ teaspoon ground paprika

1 cup (100g) pizza cheese

60g (2 ounces) baby spinach leaves

100g (3 ounces) fetta, crumbled

2 tablespoons gluten-free plain yoghurt

lemon wedges, to serve

METHOD

1 Preheat oven to 200°C/400°F.

2 Oil two oven trays, then dust with rice flour. Divide pizza dough into four portions. Roll each portion on a surface dusted with rice flour into 15cm (6-inch) rounds; place on trays. Cover; stand until needed.

3 Heat oil in a large frying pan over high heat; cook lamb, stirring, until lamb changes colour. Add spices; cook, stirring, for 2 minutes or until fragrant. Remove from heat. Cool slightly.

4 Sprinkle pizza cheese over pizza bases; top with half the spinach, then all the lamb mixture and fetta.

5 Bake pizzas for 20 minutes or until golden and cheese is melted. Just before serving, top with remaining spinach and yoghurt; squeeze with lemon.

INFO				MAKES 4
PREP + COOK TIME 45 MINUTES				
HEALTH FACTOR	GLUTEN FREE	NUT FREE		
FAT	ENERGY	CARB	PROTEIN	FIBRE
36.2g (13.3g sat)	2793kJ (667 cal)	55g	29.2g	1.4g
				PER PIZZA

TOP TIPS

Swap lamb for beef or chicken mince. If the pizza base is not crisping as much as you would like, place the cooked pizzas on an oiled, heated grill pan (or barbecue plate) for a few minutes.

MUSHROOM, CAVOLO NERO & QUINOA RISOTTO

INGREDIENTS

20g (¾ ounce) dried porcini mushrooms

½ cup (125ml) boiling water

1 tablespoon olive oil

1 medium brown onion (150g), chopped finely

2 flat mushrooms (160g), chopped coarsely

200g (6½ ounces) swiss brown mushrooms, sliced thinly

2 cloves garlic, crushed

1 cup (200g) white quinoa, rinsed, drained

1.25 litres (5 cups) gluten-free vegetable stock

2 sprigs fresh thyme

200g (6½ ounces) cavolo nero, sliced thinly

⅔ cup (50g) finely grated parmesan

METHOD

1 Place porcini mushrooms in a heatproof bowl; cover with the boiling water. Stand for 5 minutes.

2 Meanwhile, heat oil in a medium frying pan over medium heat; cook onion, stirring, for 3 minutes or until soft. Add flat and swiss brown mushrooms; cook, stirring, for 3 minutes or until browned and tender. Add garlic; cook, stirring, for 1 minute or until fragrant. Stir in quinoa, stock and thyme.

3 Remove porcini mushrooms from water (reserve the soaking liquid); chop coarsely. Add porcini mushrooms and soaking liquid to pan. Bring to the boil; simmer, uncovered for 20 minutes until liquid is absorbed and quinoa is tender. Discard thyme.

4 Add cavolo nero; stir until wilted. Remove from heat; stir through half the parmesan.

5 Serve risotto topped with remaining parmesan.

INFO   SERVES 4

PREP + COOK TIME 40 MINUTES			
HEALTH FACTOR	GLUTEN FREE	EGG FREE	NUT FREE

FAT	ENERGY	CARB	PROTEIN	FIBRE
16.9g (4.3g sat)	1743kJ (416 cal)	41g	19.7g	10.7g

PER SERVING

TOP TIPS
Crêpes can be made a day ahead; store in an airtight container. Swap pancetta for bacon or ham. Fresh ricotta is available from the deli section of supermarkets.

PANCETTA & MUSHROOM CRÊPES

These tender parcels make the perfect dish when you're craving comfort.

INGREDIENTS

1 tablespoon olive oil

1 large brown onion (200g), chopped finely

2 cloves garlic, crushed

400g (12½ ounces) canned diced tomatoes

2 tablespoons finely shredded fresh basil

200g (6½ ounces) button mushrooms, sliced thinly

50g (1½ ounces) mild pancetta, chopped coarsely

500g (1 pound) fresh ricotta

250g (8 ounces) frozen spinach, thawed, drained

1 cup (100g) coarsely grated mozzarella

GLUTEN-FREE CRÊPES

2 eggs

½ cup (65g) gluten-free plain (all-purpose) flour

¼ cup (45g) rice flour

¾ cup (180ml) milk

40g (1½ ounces) butter, melted

METHOD

1 Make gluten-free crêpes.

2 Heat half the oil in a large frying pan over medium heat; cook onion and garlic, stirring, for 5 minutes or until onion softens. Add tomatoes; cook, uncovered, over low heat, stirring occasionally, for 5 minutes or until sauce thickens slightly. Remove from heat. Cool slightly. Stir in basil; season to taste.

3 Heat remaining oil in a medium frying pan over high heat; cook mushrooms and pancetta, stirring, for 5 minutes or until softened. Transfer to a medium bowl; stir in ricotta and spinach until combined. Season.

4 Preheat oven to 180°C/350°F.

5 Spoon half the tomato sauce over the base of a 2 litre (8-cup) ovenproof dish. Spoon ricotta mixture evenly over crêpes; roll to enclose. Arrange crêpes, side-by-side, in dish. Spoon over remaining tomato sauce; sprinkle with mozzarella.

6 Bake, uncovered, for 20 minutes or until mixture is heated through and mozzarella is golden.

GLUTEN-FREE CRÊPES Whisk eggs then both flours in a medium bowl. Gradually add milk, whisking between additions until batter is smooth; season. Heat a 20cm (8-inch) (base measurement) frying pan over medium heat; brush with melted butter. Pour 2 tablespoonfuls of batter into pan; swirl to coat base. Cook for 1 minute or until golden; turn, cook for a further 30 seconds. Repeat to make a total of eight crêpes.

INFO			SERVES 4	
PREP + COOK TIME 1¼ HOURS				
HEALTH FACTOR	GLUTEN FREE	NUT FREE		

FAT	ENERGY	CARB	PROTEIN	FIBRE
39.9g (21g sat)	2667kJ (637 cal)	33.8g	34.5g	7g

PER SERVING

JERK SALMON WITH BLACK BEAN SALAD

INGREDIENTS

2 teaspoons ground coriander

1 teaspoon dried thyme

½ teaspoon ground cinnamon

½ teaspoon chilli powder

½ teaspoon ground allspice

1 clove garlic, crushed

4 x 100g (3-ounce) salmon fillets, skin and bones removed

2 trimmed corn cobs (500g)

cooking-oil spray

1 cup (200g) canned black beans, drained, rinsed

200g (6½ ounces) cherry tomatoes, halved

1 small avocado (200g), chopped

1 green onion (scallion), sliced thinly

1 cup loosely packed fresh coriander (cilantro) leaves

1 tablespoon olive oil

1 tablespoon lime juice

METHOD

1 Combine ground coriander, dried thyme, cinnamon, chilli powder, allspice and garlic in a small bowl; rub all over salmon.

2 Meanwhile, cook corn in a medium saucepan of boiling water for 6 minutes or until tender; drain. Cool.

3 Spray a large frying pan with oil; cook salmon, over medium heat, for 3 minutes each side or until just cooked.

4 Meanwhile, cut kernels from corn. Place kernels in a large bowl with beans, tomato, avocado, green onion, fresh coriander and combined oil and juice; toss gently to combine. Season to taste.

5 Serve salmon with salad, and if you like, lime wedges.

INFO   SERVES 4

PREP + COOK TIME 25 MINUTES				
HEALTH FACTOR	GLUTEN FREE	DAIRY FREE	NUT FREE	EGG FREE
FAT 22.3g (4.6g sat)	ENERGY 1819kJ (434 cal)	CARB 27g	PROTEIN 25.5g	FIBRE 13g

PER SERVING

SALMON PARCELS WITH KIPFLER POTATOES

INGREDIENTS

600g (1¼ pounds) kipfler (fingerling) potatoes, sliced thinly

1 medium red onion (170g), cut into wedges

1 tablespoon olive oil

1 lemon (140g), sliced thinly

2 small tomato (180g), sliced thinly

4 x 150g (9½-ounce) salmon fillets, skin and bones removed

1 tablespoon drained baby capers, rinsed

2 teaspoons fennel seeds

150g (4½ ounces) baby spinach leaves

½ cup firmly packed fresh flat-leaf parsley leaves

METHOD

1 Preheat oven to 200°C/400°F.

2 Combine potato and onion in a medium baking dish; drizzle with half the oil, season. Roast for 30 minutes or until browned lightly and tender.

3 Meanwhile, arrange lemon and tomato slices on two 30cm (12-inch) squares of baking paper; top with salmon, capers and seeds, drizzle with remaining oil. Fold paper into parcels to enclose salmon; place on a baking tray. Bake for 8 minutes or until salmon is cooked as you like.

4 Toss spinach through potato mixture.

5 Serve fish with potato mixture, topped with parsley.

INFO				SERVES 4
PREP + COOK TIME 50 MINUTES				
HEALTH FACTOR	GLUTEN FREE	DAIRY FREE	NUT FREE	EGG FREE

FAT	ENERGY	CARB	PROTEIN	FIBRE
15.6g (3.1g sat)	1642kJ (392 cal)	23.2g	35.5g	5g

PER SERVING

TOP TIPS

Baking the salmon in a parcel means all the flavours, juices and steam are locked in to give a moist and tasty result. You could try this recipe with firm white fish fillets or even chicken breast. The cooking time will vary depending on the thickness of the cut.

SALMON & QUINOA KOFTA WITH HERB SALAD

Kofta is a family of meatball-inspired dishes common in Middle Eastern and Balkan cooking. This version uses fresh salmon for a modern twist.

INGREDIENTS

½ cup (100g) red quinoa

1 cup (250ml) water

600g (1¼ pounds) salmon fillets, skin and bones removed, chopped coarsely

1 medium brown onion (150g), grated coarsely

2 teaspoons ground cumin

1 teaspoon ground coriander

1 teaspoon ground cinnamon

1 teaspoon ground allspice

1 tablespoon olive oil

HERB TOMATO SALAD

500g (1 pound) mixed tomato medley, sliced thickly

1 medium red onion (170g), sliced thinly

½ cup loosely packed fresh flat-leaf parsley leaves

½ cup loosely packed fresh mint leaves

2 tablespoons pomegranate molasses

2 tablespoons olive oil

METHOD

1 Rinse quinoa under cold running water until liquid runs clear; drain well. Place quinoa in a medium saucepan with the water; bring to the boil. Reduce heat to low; cook, covered, for 15 minutes or until liquid is absorbed. Cool.

2 Meanwhile, make herb tomato salad.

3 Blend or process salmon until finely chopped; transfer to a medium bowl. Add quinoa, onion and spices; season, stir to combine. Shape mixture into 12 oval shapes.

4 Heat oil in a large frying pan over medium heat; cook kofta, in two batches, turning, for 3 minutes or until golden brown and just cooked through. Remove from pan, cover; rest for 5 minutes.

5 Serve kofta with herb tomato salad.

HERB TOMATO SALAD Place tomatoes, onion and herbs in a large bowl with combined pomegranate molasses and oil; toss to combine, season to taste.

INFO					SERVES 4
PREP + COOK TIME 45 MINUTES (+ COOLING)					
HEALTH FACTOR	GLUTEN FREE	DAIRY FREE	NUT FREE	YEAST FREE	EGG FREE
FAT 16.2g(2.6g sat)	ENERGY 1556kJ (372 cal)	CARB 35g	PROTEIN 19.2g	FIBRE 5.1g	
				PER SERVING	

TOP TIPS

We used red quinoa in this recipe, but you could use the white variety if you prefer.

SOUTHERN BUFFALO-STYLE CHICKEN WINGS

INGREDIENTS

16 chicken wings (2kg)

1 cup (180g) rice flour

$\frac{1}{3}$ cup (95g) gluten-free tomato sauce (ketchup)

$\frac{1}{4}$ cup (70g) gluten-free barbecue sauce

$1\frac{1}{2}$ tablespoons white vinegar

1 teaspoon chilli flakes

TOMATO AVOCADO SALSA

2 large tomatoes (500g), chopped coarsely

1 large avocado (320g), chopped coarsely

2 tablespoons lemon juice

$\frac{1}{3}$ cup coarsely chopped fresh coriander (cilantro)

METHOD

1 Preheat oven to 220°C/425°F. Oil two wire racks; place over two large baking trays.

2 Cut wings into three pieces at the joints; discard wing tips. Toss wings in rice flour; place on wire racks. Bake, uncovered, for 40 minutes, turning once during cooking, until golden brown and cooked through.

3 Meanwhile, make tomato avocado salsa.

4 Place sauces, vinegar and chilli flakes in a small saucepan; cook, stirring, over

medium heat, until hot. Transfer sauce to a large bowl. Add hot chicken; turn until coated evenly.

5 Serve chicken with tomato avocado salsa.

TOMATO AVOCADO SALSA Combine ingredients in a medium bowl.

INFO				SERVES 4
PREP + COOK TIME 25 MINUTES				
HEALTH FACTOR	GLUTEN FREE	DAIRY FREE	NUT FREE	EGG FREE
FAT	ENERGY	CARB	PROTEIN	FIBRE
75.3g (21.2g sat)	5507kJ (1315 cal)	72.7g	77.2g	22.1g

PER SERVING

• TOP TIPS

To save time, ask the butcher to remove the wing tips and cut the wings into two pieces. If you don't want spicy wings, add less chilli flakes, or omit the chilli altogether if serving for the whole family. This recipe is best made just before serving.

SALT & PEPPER SQUID

INGREDIENTS

2 tablespoons sea salt

2 tablespoons black peppercorns

1½ teaspoons dried chilli flakes

¼ cup (35g) 100% corn (maize) cornflour (cornstarch)

vegetable oil, for deep-frying

750g (1½ pounds) cleaned squid hoods, sliced thickly, tentacles reserved

125g (4 ounces) mixed baby salad leaves

1 lebanese cucumber (130g), halved, sliced thinly

½ cup loosely packed fresh coriander (cilantro) leaves

½ small red onion (50g), sliced thinly

1 small carrot (70g), cut into matchsticks

1 tablespoon rice wine vinegar

2 teaspoons light olive oil

METHOD

1 Crush salt, peppercorns and chilli with a mortar and pestle; combine with cornflour in a medium bowl.

2 Heat vegetable oil in a heavy-based saucepan, over medium-high heat, until oil reaches 190°C/375°F on a sugar (candy) thermometer (or when a cube of bread turns golden in about 10 seconds).

3 Coat squid in cornflour mixture; shake off excess. Deep-fry squid, in batches, for 3 minutes or until browned lightly

and cooked through. Drain on paper towel; cover to keep warm.

4 Place salad leaves and remaining ingredients in a large bowl; toss gently to combine. Serve squid with salad and, if you like, lemon wedges.

INFO					SERVES 4
PREP + COOK TIME 35 MINUTES					
HEALTH FACTOR	GLUTEN FREE	DAIRY FREE	NUT FREE	YEAST FREE	EGG FREE

FAT	ENERGY	CARB	PROTEIN	FIBRE
15.6g (2.4g sat)	1213kJ (290 cal)	11.3g	32.6g	2.9g

PER SERVING

TOP TIPS

To save you time, ask the fishmonger to clean the squid hoods for you. This recipe is best made just before serving.

TOP TIPS

Omit the rice and serve the beef and pickle mixtures in lettuce leaves, if you like. To cook your own brown rice you will need to boil ¾ cup (150g) brown rice in water for 25 minutes or until tender; drain well.

BEEF & RICE STIR-FRY WITH CARROT & CUCUMBER PICKLE

Inspired with Asian flavours, this healthy and convenient dish makes a quick and easy mid-week meal the whole family will love.

INGREDIENTS

500g (1-pound) packet microwave brown rice

2 tablespoons olive oil

4 eggs, beaten lightly

1 clove garlic, crushed

1 tablespoon grated fresh ginger

400g (12½ ounces) lean minced (ground) beef

1 tablespoon gluten-free oyster sauce

4 cups (320g) shredded cabbage

⅓ cup shredded fresh mint leaves

2 green onions (scallions), sliced thinly

CARROT & CUCUMBER PICKLE

⅔ cup (160ml) rice wine vinegar

⅓ cup (75g) caster (superfine) sugar

¼ teaspoon dried chilli flakes

1 medium carrot (120g), cut into matchsticks

2 lebanese cucumbers (260g), seeded, cut into matchsticks

METHOD

1 Cook rice according to packet instructions.

2 Make carrot & cucumber pickle.

3 Heat 1 teaspoon of the oil in a wok over high heat; add a quarter of the egg, swirl wok to make a thin omelette. Cook, uncovered, until egg is just set. Remove from wok; roll tightly, cut into thick strips. Repeat using 3 teaspoons of the oil and remaining egg to make three more omelettes. Roll tightly; cut into thick strips.

4 Heat remaining oil in wok over high heat; stir-fry garlic and ginger until fragrant. Add beef; cook, stirring, until beef is browned. Add sauce; stir-fry until heated through. Remove from wok.

5 Stir-fry cabbage in wok (add a little water if needed) until tender. Return beef to wok with rice and mint; stir-fry until hot.

6 Drain carrot and cucumber pickle; serve rice topped with pickle, omelette and onion.

CARROT & CUCUMBER PICKLE Combine vinegar, sugar and chilli flakes in a small bowl until sugar dissolves. Add carrot and cucumber; toss to combine.

INFO			SERVES 4	
PREP + COOK TIME 20 MINUTES				
HEALTH FACTOR	GLUTEN FREE	DAIRY FREE	NUT FREE	
FAT 21.8g (6.1g)	ENERGY 2339kJ (559 cal)	CARB 51.5g	PROTEIN 35.5g	FIBRE 6.7g

PER SERVING

SWEETS

There's no reason to give up on tasty treats with these scrumptious recipes. From delectable desserts to sweet, dainty cupcakes and biscuits, these gluten-free pleasures will delight even the most fervent sweet tooth. The recipes in this section are also free of nuts and many are also dairy and egg-free, making the ideal indulgence for those with allergies.

LEMONTONS

INGREDIENTS

4 eggs

⅔ cup (150g) caster (superfine) sugar

⅓ cup (50g) 100% corn (maize) cornflour (cornstarch)

⅓ cup (45g) gluten-free self-raising flour

⅓ cup (45g) gluten-free plain (all-purpose) flour

1 cup (250ml) store-bought gluten-free lemon curd

1½ cups (240g) gluten-free icing sugar (pure confectioners' sugar)

⅓ cup (80ml) lemon juice

½ cup (125ml) boiling water

3 cups (300g) shredded coconut

METHOD

1 Preheat oven to 180°C/350°F. Grease a deep 23cm (9-inch) square cake pan; line base with baking paper.

2 Beat eggs and caster sugar in a large bowl with an electric mixer for 8 minutes or until mixture is thick and creamy.

3 Triple sift flours. Whisk flour mixture into egg mixture until just combined. Pour mixture into pan.

4 Bake cake for 25 minutes or until cake is dry to the touch and edges are coming away from the sides of the pan. Stand cake in pan for 5 minutes before turning, top-side up, onto a wire rack to cool completely.

5 Combine lemon curd, sifted icing sugar, juice and the water in a large bowl until well combined. Place coconut on a large plate or in a wide bowl.

6 Cut cake into 16 squares. Use two forks to dip squares, one at a time, into lemon mixture until coated all over; toss in coconut. Place on a wire rack until firm.

INFO   MAKES 16

PREP + COOK TIME 1 HOUR (+ STANDING)				
HEALTH FACTOR	GLUTEN FREE	YEAST FREE	NUT FREE	
FAT	ENERGY	CARB	PROTEIN	FIBRE
16.5g (11.1g sat)	1239kJ (296 cal)	41.8g	3.6g	2.9g

PER LEMONTON

TOP TIPS

Lemontons can be made a day ahead; store in an airtight container. You can make strawberry lemontons by dipping the sponge into gluten-free strawberry topping and coating in coconut tinted with pink food colouring.

DARK CHOCOLATE CHEESECAKE BROWNIE

INGREDIENTS

dairy-free spread, for greasing

150g (4½ ounces) dairy-free dark chocolate, chopped coarsely

150g (4½ ounces) dairy-free spread

1¼ cups (275g) caster (superfine) sugar

2 eggs, beaten lightly

2 teaspoons vanilla extract

½ cup (65g) gluten-free self-raising flour

½ cup (60g) tapioca flour

⅓ cup (35g) dutch-processed cocoa

227g (7 ounces) tofutti better than cream cheese, softened (see top tips)

1 tablespoon caster (superfine) sugar, extra

METHOD

1 Preheat oven to 160°C/325°F. Grease a deep 22cm (9-inch) square cake pan with dairy-free spread; line base and sides with baking paper.

2 Stir chocolate and dairy-free spread in a medium saucepan over low heat for 5 minutes or until chocolate melts and mixture is smooth. Remove from heat. Cool for 5 minutes.

3 Stir sugar into chocolate mixture; add eggs and half the extract, stir to combine. Stir in sifted flours and cocoa until combined. Pour mixture into pan.

4 Combine tofutti, extra sugar and remaining extract in a small bowl. Drop large spoonfuls of tofutti mixture over chocolate mixture. Use a knife to gently swirl the mixtures together to create a marbled effect.

5 Bake brownie for 1¼ hours or until a skewer inserted in the centre comes out clean. Cool brownie in pan before cutting into 24 squares.

TOP TIPS

'Tofutti better than cream cheese' is a tofu-based dairy-free cream cheese substitute, available in the refrigerated section of health food stores and most major supermarkets.

INFO				MAKES 24
PREP + COOK TIME 1¾ HOURS (+ COOLING)				
HEALTH FACTOR	GLUTEN FREE	DAIRY FREE	NUT FREE	YEAST FREE

FAT	ENERGY	CARB	PROTEIN	FIBRE
10g (3.3g sat)	755kJ (180 cal)	21.5g	1.5g	0.4g

PER PIECE

BLUEBERRY & WHITE CHOCOLATE SCONES

Afternoon tea isn't complete without scones. These decadent treats combine the tastiest ingredients for a little luxury feasting.

You need a 5cm (2-inch) round cutter.

INGREDIENTS

3 cups (405g) gluten-free
   self-raising flour

1 tablespoon caster (superfine) sugar

2 teaspoons gluten-free baking powder

125g (4 ounces) fresh blueberries

180g (5½ ounces) white chocolate,
   chopped coarsely

1¼ cups (310ml) milk

1 tablespoon gluten-free icing sugar
   (pure confectioners' sugar)

⅓ cup (80g) blueberry jam

½ cup (125ml) crème fraîche

METHOD

1 Preheat oven to 220°C/425°F. Line a baking tray with baking paper.

2 Sift flour, sugar and baking powder into a large bowl. Add blueberries and chocolate; stir to combine. Make a well in the centre, add milk; stir until just combined.

3 Turn dough onto a lightly gluten-free floured surface; pat out until 3cm (1¼ inches) thick. Cut out 5cm (2-inch) rounds. Place scones, just touching, on tray. Gently knead scraps of dough together; repeat process to get 16 rounds.

4 Bake scones for 15 minutes or until browned lightly and cooked through (they should sound hollow when tapped). Dust with sifted icing sugar; serve immediately with jam and crème fraîche.

INFO   MAKES 16

PREP + COOK TIME 30 MINUTES				
HEALTH FACTOR	GLUTEN FREE	YEAST FREE	NUT FREE	EGG FREE
FAT 7.3g (4.6g sat)	ENERGY 898kJ (214 cal)	CARB 35.5g	PROTEIN 2g	FIBRE 0.3g

PER SCONE

TOP TIPS ●

Depending on the brand of flour you use, you may need to add extra flour. The scone dough should feel soft and slightly sticky to the touch. These scones are best served on the day they are made and are best eaten warm. You can use your favourite jam to serve with the scones.

RASPBERRY & LEMON SYRUP CAKE

Don't miss out on a family favourite. This beautiful raspberry and lemon syrup cake is free of wheat and dairy, but still tastes incredible!

INGREDIENTS

dairy-free spread, for greasing

rice flour, for dusting

125g (4 ounces) dairy-free spread

¾ cup (165g) caster (superfine) sugar

1 tablespoon finely grated lemon rind

3 eggs

1¾ cups (235g) gluten-free self-raising flour

¼ cup (60ml) soy milk

¾ cup (100g) frozen raspberries

LEMON SYRUP

1 tablespoon finely grated lemon rind

½ cup (110g) caster (superfine) sugar

¼ cup (60ml) lemon juice

¼ cup (60ml) water

METHOD

1 Preheat oven to 190°C/375°F. Grease a 21cm (8½-inch) baba pan well with dairy-free spread; dust with rice flour, shake out excess.

2 Beat dairy-free spread, sugar and rind in a medium bowl with an electric mixer until light and fluffy. Beat in eggs, one at a time, until just combined. Stir in sifted flour and milk, alternately, in batches. Stir in raspberries. Spread mixture into pan.

3 Bake cake for about 45 minutes.

4 Just before cake is cooked, make lemon syrup.

5 Stand cake in pan for 5 minutes before turning onto a wire rack over a tray. Pour hot syrup over hot cake.

LEMON SYRUP Stir ingredients in a small saucepan over heat, without boiling, until sugar dissolves. Bring to the boil. Reduce heat; simmer, uncovered, without stirring, for 5 minutes or until syrup thickens slightly.

SERVING SUGGESTION Serve with vanilla soy ice-cream or vanilla bean soy yoghurt.

TOP TIPS

If you have a zesting tool, use it to make thin strips of lemon rind for serving. The cake is best served on the day of baking. Reheat cold cake slices in a microwave oven on medium (50%) until heated through.

INFO			SERVES 8
PREP + COOK TIME 1¼ HOURS			
HEALTH FACTOR	GLUTEN FREE	DAIRY FREE	NUT FREE

FAT	ENERGY	CARB	PROTEIN	FIBRE
13.3g (3.3g sat)	1570kJ (375 cal)	61g	3.6g	1g

PER SERVING

CHOCOLATE CARAMEL SLICE

INGREDIENTS

⅔ cup (90g) gluten-free plain (all-purpose) flour

⅓ cup (75g) firmly packed brown sugar

⅓ cup (25g) desiccated coconut

85g (3 ounces) butter, melted

395g (12½ ounces) canned sweetened condensed milk

1 tablespoon golden syrup

40g (1½ ounces) butter, extra

150g (4½ ounces) dark (semi-sweet) chocolate, chopped coarsely

METHOD

1 Preheat oven to 180°C/350°F. Grease a 19cm (8-inch) square cake pan; line base and sides with baking paper, extending the paper 5cm (2 inches) above sides.

2 Combine sifted flour, sugar and coconut in a medium bowl; stir in melted butter until combined. Spoon into pan; use the back of a spoon to press mixture evenly over base of pan.

3 Bake base for 15 minutes or until golden. Cool.

4 Place condensed milk, syrup and half of the extra butter in a medium saucepan; cook over medium heat, stirring constantly, for 10 minutes or until caramel is thickened and a golden colour. Pour over base; cool in pan.

5 Place chocolate and remaining extra butter in a medium heatproof bowl over a medium saucepan of simmering water (don't let water touch base of bowl); stir until chocolate melts. Pour chocolate mixture over caramel layer. Cool slice completely before cutting.

INFO				MAKES 20
PREP + COOK TIME 40 MINUTES (+ COOLING)				
HEALTH FACTOR	GLUTEN FREE	YEAST FREE	NUT FREE	EGG FREE
FAT 10.4g (6.8g sat)	ENERGY 873kJ (209 cal)	CARB 27.4g	PROTEIN 2.7g	FIBRE 0.3g
				PER PIECE

• TOP TIPS

Make an upside-down caramel slice by adding 2 tablespoons of cocoa powder to the biscuit base and replacing the dark chocolate with white chocolate. The slice can be made 1 week ahead; store covered in the fridge.

RASPBERRY & VANILLA YOGHURT ICE-BLOCKS

INGREDIENTS

¼ cup (55g) low-GI cane sugar

1 vanilla bean, split lengthways

¾ cup (180ml) water

300g (9½ ounces) frozen raspberries

750g (1½ pounds) low-fat gluten-free plain yoghurt

14 popsicle sticks

METHOD

1 Stir sugar, vanilla bean and the water in a small saucepan over low heat for 4 minutes or until sugar is dissolved. Bring to the boil, without stirring. Reduce heat; simmer for 10 minutes or until syrupy. Discard vanilla bean; cool syrup.

2 Blend cooled syrup and raspberries until smooth. Very gently swirl in yoghurt. Pour mixture into 14 x ⅓ cup (80ml) ice-block moulds. Cover moulds with a double layer of plastic wrap; this will help to keep the popsicle sticks upright. Pierce plastic with a small knife, then push popsicle sticks into each hole. Freeze overnight or until firm.

TOP TIPS

Don't stir the yoghurt into the raspberry mixture or you will lose the marbled effect. It will swirl naturally when you pour the mixture into the moulds. Use a skewer to swirl it once in the moulds, if necessary. You could use frozen strawberries, cherries or mango.

INFO				MAKES 14
PREP + COOK TIME 25 MINUTES (+ COOLING & FREEZING)				
HEALTH FACTOR	GLUTEN FREE	EGG FREE	NUT FREE	

FAT	ENERGY	CARB	PROTEIN	FIBRE
0.2g (0.1g sat)	229kJ (55 cal)	8.3g	3.5g	1.3g

PER ICE-BLOC

PASSIONFRUIT SHORTBREAD WITH PASSIONFRUIT GLAZE

These tangy biscuits are a cookie jar favourite and make a great sweet gift for special occasions and celebrations.

You need a 5cm (2-inch) heart-shaped cutter.

INGREDIENTS

125g (4 ounces) cold butter, chopped coarsely

¼ cup (55g) caster (superfine) sugar

¾ cup (75g) rice flour

¾ cup (80g) gluten-free plain (all-purpose) flour

2 tablespoons gluten-free icing sugar (pure confectioners' sugar)

1 tablespoon xanthum gum

1 tablespoon passionfruit pulp

PASSIONFRUIT GLAZE

1 teaspoon (5g) softened butter

½ cup (80g) gluten-free icing sugar (pure confectioners' sugar)

2 tablespoons passionfruit pulp

TOP TIPS

Store shortbread in an airtight container in the fridge for up to 2 weeks. Swap passionfruit for 2 teaspoons of finely grated lemon or orange rind for a citrus-flavoured shortbread.

METHOD

1 Preheat oven to 150°C/300°F. Grease two oven trays; line with baking paper.

2 Beat butter and caster sugar in a small bowl with an electric mixer until just combined; gradually beat in the combined sifted flours, icing sugar and xanthum gum. Stir in passionfruit pulp.

3 Turn dough onto a lightly rice-floured surface; knead until just smooth. Roll out dough until 5mm (¼ inch) thick; using the heart cutter, cut 36 hearts from dough. Place hearts, about 2.5cm (1 inch) apart, on trays.

4 Bake shortbread for 15 minutes or until browned lightly and just firm. Stand on trays for 5 minutes before transferring to wire racks to cool.

5 Meanwhile, make passionfruit glaze.

6 Spread one side of the hearts with passionfruit glaze. Stand on wire racks until set.

PASSIONFRUIT GLAZE Stir ingredients in a small bowl until smooth.

INFO			MAKES 36
PREP + COOK TIME 1 HOUR			

HEALTH FACTOR	GLUTEN FREE	EGG FREE	NUT FREE

FAT	ENERGY	CARB	PROTEIN	FIBRE
3g (2g sat)	251kJ (60 cal)	8.1g	0.2g	0.3g

PER SHORTBREAD

RED VELVET WHOOPIE PIES WITH ORANGE FILLING

Whoopie pies are a classic American dessert, made from two round mound-shaped pieces of chocolate cake with a creamy filling.

INGREDIENTS

dairy-free spread, for greasing

75g (2½ ounces) dairy-free spread

⅓ cup (75g) caster (superfine) sugar

1 egg

¾ cup (100g) gluten-free self-raising flour

1 tablespoon gluten-free baby rice cereal

1 tablespoon cocoa powder

¼ cup (60ml) soy milk

1 teaspoon red food colouring

½ cup (120g) tofutti better than cream cheese, softened (see top tips)

1 tablespoon caster (superfine) sugar, extra

1 teaspoon finely grated orange rind

1 tablespoon gluten-free icing sugar (pure confectioners' sugar)

METHOD

1 Preheat oven to 160°C/325°F. Grease two 12-hole (1 tablespoon/20ml) shallow round-based patty pans with dairy-free spread.

2 Beat dairy-free spread and sugar in a medium bowl with an electric mixer until combined. Beat in egg until combined. Stir in the sifted flour, rice cereal and cocoa, and milk, alternately, stirring after each addition. Stir in colouring. Drop rounded teaspoons of mixture into pan holes; smooth tops.

3 Bake cakes for 8 minutes or until cooked through. Transfer to a wire rack to cool.

4 Combine tofutti, extra sugar and rind in a small bowl. Sandwich cakes with filling. Just before serving, dust whoopie pies with sifted icing sugar.

INFO				MAKES 12
PREP + COOK TIME 30 MINUTES (+ COOLING)				
HEALTH FACTOR	GLUTEN FREE	DAIRY FREE	NUT FREE	YEAST FREE
FAT 8g (2g sat)	ENERGY 575kJ (137 cal)	CARB 14.4g	PROTEIN 2.1g	FIBRE 0.5g

PER WHOOPIE PIE

TOP TIPS

'Tofutti better than cream cheese' is a tofu-based dairy-free cream cheese substitute, available in the refrigerated section of health food stores and most major supermarkets. If you are not dairy intolerant, you can replace the dairy-free spread with butter and the tofutti with cream cheese.

VANILLA CUPCAKES

Sweet and simple, enjoy these bite-sized cakes plain or use the recipe as the base for tasty fruit-filled varieties – best served on the day of baking.

INGREDIENTS

1 cup (220g) caster (superfine) sugar

1 teaspoon vanilla extract

3 eggs

125g (4 ounces) dairy-free spread

1½ cups gluten-free self-raising flour

½ cup gluten-free baby rice cereal

¼ cup soy milk

VANILLA FROSTING

125g (4 ounces) dairy-free spread

1 teaspoon vanilla extract

1½ cups gluten-free icing sugar (pure confectioners' sugar)

2 teaspoons soy milk

METHOD

1 Preheat oven to 180°C/350°F. Line 14 holes of two 12-hole (⅓-cup/80ml) muffin pans with paper cases.

2 Beat sugar, vanilla and eggs in a small bowl with an electric mixer for 5 minutes or until thick and pale. Add dairy-free spread, a little at a time, beating well between additions. Gradually add sifted flour, rice cereal and milk. Spoon mixture into paper cases.

3 Bake cupcakes for 20 minutes. Leave cupcakes in pan or 5 minutes before turning, top-side up, onto a wire rack to cool.

4 Meanwhile, make vanilla frosting.

5 Spread frosting over cooled cupcakes.

VANILLA FROSTING Beat dairy-free spread and vanilla in a small bowl with an electric mixer until pale. Beat in sifted icing sugar and milk, in two batches, until well combined and smooth.

VARIATIONS

Blueberry cupcakes Stir in ¾ cup frozen blueberries to vanilla cupcake mixture after adding the soy milk.

Coconut cherry cupcakes Stir in ¼ cup desiccated coconut, ½ cup sifted cocoa powder, ¼ cup soy milk, 100g (3 ounces) finely chopped red glacé cherries and ¼ cup finely chopped dairy-free dark chocolate into the vanilla cupcake mixture after adding the baby rice cereal. Make vanilla frosting recipe, with the following changes: Combine 1 cup sifted gluten-free icing sugar (pure confectioners' sugar) and ½ cup sifted cocoa powder; beat combined sifted mixture with the 2 teaspoons of soy milk, in two batches, until combined and smooth. Spread over cupcakes.

Apple cinnamon cupcakes Stir in ⅓ cup canned pie apple into the vanilla cupcake mixture after adding the soy milk. Combine 2 teaspoons ground cinnamon and 2 tablespoons gluten-free icing sugar (pure confectioners' sugar); dust cupcakes with cinnamon mix.

INFO

MAKES 14

PREP + COOK TIME	45 MINUTES (+ COOLING)		

HEALTH FACTOR	GLUTEN FREE	DAIRY FREE	NUT FREE

FAT	ENERGY	CARB	PROTEIN	FIBRE
13.9g (3.4g sat)	1250kJ (299 cal)	43.2g	1.9g	0.1g

PER CUPCAKE

SPECIAL OCCASIONS

Food is an integral part of many important celebrations, and whether it's a stand-out cake or traditional seasonal treat, following a gluten-free diet doesn't mean you need to miss out. From luscious chocolate cakes to tangy fruit delights and cool summer desserts, these special occasion desserts will be the star attraction at your next event.

WHOLE ORANGE CAKE

Free from gluten, nuts and dairy, this delicious citrus cake is sure to impress guests at your next dinner party or get-together.

INGREDIENTS

dairy-free spread, for greasing

2 large oranges (600g), unpeeled

3 eggs

1 cup (220g) caster (superfine) sugar

125g (4 ounces) dairy-free spread

1 cup (135g) gluten-free self raising flour

½ cup (65g) gluten-free plain (all-purpose) flour

¾ cup (50g) gluten-free baby rice cereal

ORANGE SYRUP

1 cup (220g) caster (superfine) sugar

⅔ cup (160ml) orange juice

⅓ cup (80ml) water

3 medium oranges (720g), segmented (see top tip)

METHOD

1 Preheat oven to 180°C/350°F. Grease a deep 20cm (8-inch) round cake pan with dairy-free spread; line base and sides with baking paper.

2 Place unpeeled oranges in a medium saucepan; cover with water. Bring to the boil; boil, uncovered, for 2 minutes, drain.

3 Return oranges to same pan; cover with water and repeat step 2, two more times. Drain oranges; cool. Coarsely chop oranges; discard seeds. Blend or process rind and flesh until finely chopped.

4 Beat eggs and sugar in a small bowl with an electric mixer until thick and pale. Add dairy-free spread, a little at a time, beating well between additions. Gradually add sifted flours, rice cereal and 1½ cups of the processed orange (discard any remaining mixture). Spread mixture into pan.

5 Bake cake for 50 minutes. Stand cake in pan for 5 minutes.

6 Meanwhile, make orange syrup.

7 Turn cake, top-side up, onto a wire rack over a tray; pour hot syrup over hot cake. Serve topped with reserved orange segments.

ORANGE SYRUP Stir sugar, juice and the water in a small saucepan, over heat, without boiling until sugar is dissolved; bring to the boil. Reduce heat; simmer, uncovered, without stirring, for 5 minutes or until thickened slightly. Stir in orange segments. Pour syrup into a heatproof jug; reserve orange segments.

SERVING SUGGESTION Serve with dairy-free ice-cream.

INFO				SERVES 8
PREP + COOK TIME 1½ HOURS (+ COOLING)				
HEALTH FACTOR	GLUTEN FREE	DAIRY FREE	NUT FREE	
FAT	ENERGY	CARB	PROTEIN	FIBRE
13.3g (3.3g sat)	2060kJ (492 cal)	89.4g	4.6g	2.9g
				PER SERVING

TOP TIP
To segment the oranges, cut off the rind with the white pith, following the curve of the fruit. Cut down either side of each segment close to the membrane to release the segment.

FRUIT MINCE PIES

A long-held Christmas tradition, these festive treats date as far back
as the 13th Century and have a Middle Eastern origin.

*The fruit mixture needs to marinate for
2 days. You will need a 7cm (2¾-inch)
round cutter and a 5cm (2-inch) star
cutter for this recipe.*

INGREDIENTS

⅔ cup (110g) sultanas

⅔ cup (110g) dried currants

⅔ cup (100g) raisins, chopped coarsely

⅓ cup (55g) mixed peel

⅓ cup (45g) dried cranberries

⅓ cup (50g) finely chopped dried dates

¼ cup (45g) finely chopped prunes

1 large apple (200g), peeled,
  grated coarsely

⅓ cup (75g) firmly packed brown sugar

¼ cup (85g) marmalade

2 tablespoons dark rum

½ teaspoon ground cinnamon

½ teaspoon mixed spice

1 roll (400g) packaged sweet vanilla
  bean gluten-free shortcrust pastry

2 tablespoons gluten-free icing sugar
  (pure confectioners' sugar)

METHOD

1 Combine fruit, brown sugar, marmalade, rum and spices
in a large glass bowl. Cover; stand at room temperature for
2 days, stirring occasionally.

2 Preheat oven to 180°C/350°F. Grease two 12-hole
(1-tablespoon/20ml) shallow round-based patty pans.

3 Roll out pastry on a surface dusted with a little gluten-free
flour until 3mm (⅛-inch) thick. Cut 24 x 7cm (2¾-inch) rounds
from pastry, re-rolling scraps as necessary. Press pastry rounds
into pan holes.

4 Roll remaining pastry scraps until 3mm (⅛-inch) thick.
Cut 24 x 5cm (2-inch) stars from pastry, re-rolling scraps
as necessary.

5 Spoon 1 tablespoon of fruit mince into each pastry case;
top each with a pastry star.

6 Bake pies for 20 minutes or until browned lightly. Cool
in pans. Dust with sifted gluten-free icing sugar.

TOP TIPS

Sweet gluten-free
shortcrust pastry
comes in 400g
(12½-ounce) cylindrical
blocks; it is available
in the freezer section
of most major
supermarkets. Mince
pies will keep in an
airtight container for
up to 2 weeks.

INFO				MAKES 24
PREP + COOK TIME 40 MINUTES (+ STANDING & COOLING)				
HEALTH FACTOR	GLUTEN FREE	YEAST FREE	NUT FREE	EGG FREE

FAT	ENERGY	CARB	PROTEIN	FIBRE
5.2g (3.2g sat)	776kJ (492 cal)	32.2g	1.5g	1.3g
				PER PIE

CHOCOLATE MUD CAKE WITH WHITE CHOCOLATE GANACHE

This self-indulgent cake can also be covered with dark chocolate ganache if you prefer. Serve with whipped cream or ice-cream. Yum!

INGREDIENTS

250g (8 ounces) butter, chopped coarsely

200g (6½ ounces) dark (semi-sweet) chocolate, chopped coarsely

2 cups (440g) caster (superfine) sugar

1 cup (250ml) milk

2 teaspoons instant coffee granules

1 cup (135g) gluten-free plain (all-purpose) flour

1 cup (135g) gluten-free self-raising flour

½ cup (90g) rice flour

¼ cup (20g) gluten-free baby rice cereal

¼ cup (25g) cocoa powder

2 eggs

WHITE CHOCOLATE GANACHE

450g (14½ ounces) white chocolate, chopped coarsely

¾ cup (180ml) thickened (heavy) cream

METHOD

1 Grease a deep 22cm (9-inch) round cake pan; line base and side with baking paper.

2 Stir butter, chocolate, sugar, milk and coffee in a large saucepan over low heat for 5 minutes or until chocolate melts and mixture is smooth. Remove from heat; cool for 5 minutes.

3 Whisk sifted flours, rice cereal and cocoa into chocolate mixture. Add eggs, whisk until combined. Pour mixture into pan; stand for 30 minutes.

4 Meanwhile, preheat oven to 160°C/325°F.

5 Bake cake about 1½ hours. Cool in pan.

6 Meanwhile, make white chocolate ganache.

7 Place cake on a serving plate or cake stand; spread ganache on top of cake.

WHITE CHOCOLATE GANACHE Place chocolate and cream in a small heatproof bowl over a small saucepan of simmering water (don't let water touch base of bowl); stir until chocolate melts and mixture is smooth. Refrigerate, stirring occasionally, for 30 minutes or until ganache is of a spreadable consistency.

INFO			SERVES 16	
PREP + COOK TIME 1¾ HOURS (+ STANDING & COOLING)				
HEALTH FACTOR	GLUTEN FREE	NUT FREE		
FAT	ENERGY	CARB	PROTEIN	FIBRE
31.2g (19.6g sat)	2412kJ (576 cal)	71.3g	5.4g	0.7g
				PER SERVING

STEAMED CHRISTMAS PUDDING

There's no need to miss out on all the trimmings at Christmas with this twist on the traditional pud, free from gluten, dairy and nuts.

The fruit mixture needs to stand overnight.

INGREDIENTS

750g (1½ pounds) dried mixed fruit

1 large green apple (200g), peeled, grated coarsely

½ cup (125ml) dry sherry

1 tablespoon finely grated orange rind

2 teaspoons mixed spice

1 teaspoon ground cinnamon

dairy-free spread, for greasing

125g (4 ounces) dairy-free spread

½ cup (110g) firmly packed brown sugar

2 eggs

2 cups (140g) stale gluten-free breadcrumbs

½ cup (65g) gluten-free plain (all-purpose) flour

½ cup (60g) tapioca flour

METHOD

1 Combine mixed fruit, apple, sherry, rind, mixed spice and cinnamon in a large bowl. Cover with plastic wrap; stand at room temperature overnight.

2 Grease a 2-litre (8-cup) pudding basin or steamer. Line base with a small round of baking paper. Place a 30cm x 40cm (12-inch x 16-inch) piece of baking paper on top of a piece of foil cut to the same size; fold a 5cm (2-inch) pleat crossways through the centre.

3 Beat dairy-free spread and sugar in a small bowl with an electric mixer until pale. Beat in eggs, one at a time. Stir egg mixture into fruit mixture. Add breadcrumbs and combined sifted flours; stir to combine. Spoon mixture into basin; top with the pleated baking paper and foil (this allows pudding to expand as it cooks); secure with kitchen string (or the lid).

4 Place an inverted saucer in the base of a large saucepan; place pudding basin on the saucer. Pour enough boiling water into the pan to come halfway up the side of the basin; cover with a tight-fitting lid. Boil pudding for 6 hours, replenishing with boiling water as necessary to maintain water level.

5 Remove pudding basin from water. Stand pudding for 10 minutes before turning out. If you like, serve topped with dried figs and drizzled with golden syrup.

INFO SERVES 12

PREP + COOK TIME	7 HOURS (+ STANDING)		
HEALTH FACTOR	GLUTEN FREE	DAIRY FREE	NUT FREE

FAT	ENERGY	CARB	PROTEIN	FIBRE
8.3g (1.9g sat)	1547kJ (369 cal)	67.3g	3.5g	4.5g

PER SERVING

TOP TIPS

The pudding can be made 1 week ahead; store, covered, in the fridge, or freeze for up to 3 months. To reheat frozen pudding, thaw for 3 days in the fridge; remove from fridge 12 hours before reheating. Discard plastic wrap and return pudding to pudding basin. Steam for 2 hours following instructions in step 4.

LEMON MERINGUE CAKE

A light and fluffy topping with a tangy sponge centre, this show-stopper will please any crowd when it comes to serving up something special.

You need a sugar (candy) thermometer.

INGREDIENTS

dairy-free spread, for greasing

3 eggs

¾ cup (165g) caster (superfine) sugar

1 tablespoon finely grated lemon rind

125g (3 ounces) dairy-free spread

1¾ cups (235g) gluten-free
self-raising flour

¾ cup (180ml) soy milk

1 cup (320g) gluten-free lemon curd

MERINGUE FROSTING

1 cup (220g) caster (superfine) sugar

⅓ cup (80ml) water

3 eggs whites

CANDIED LEMON PEEL

2 medium lemons (280g)

¼ cup (55g) caster (superfine) sugar

¼ cup (60ml) water

INFO			SERVES 12	
PREP + COOK TIME 1½ HOURS (+ COOLING & REFRIGERATION)				
HEALTH FACTOR	GLUTEN FREE	NUT FREE		
FAT 13.4g (3.3g sat)	ENERGY 1746kJ (417 cal)	CARB 72g	PROTEIN 3.8g	FIBRE 0.2g

PER SERVING

METHOD

1 Preheat oven to 180°C/350°F. Grease a deep 20cm (8-inch) round cake pan with dairy-free spread; line base and side with baking paper.

2 Beat eggs, sugar and rind in a medium bowl with an electric mixer until thick and creamy. Add dairy-free spread, a little at a time, beating until just combined. Gently whisk in sifted flour and milk, in batches, until smooth. Pour mixture into pan.

3 Bake cake for 45 minutes. Stand in pan for 5 minutes before turning, top-side up, onto a wire rack to cool.

4 Split cooled cake in half. Place one cake layer on a serving plate, cut-side up; spread with lemon curd, top with remaining cake layer. Refrigerate 30 minutes.

5 Meanwhile, make meringue frosting, then candied lemon peel.

6 Spread meringue frosting all over cake; decorate with candied lemon peel.

MERINGUE FROSTING Stir sugar and the water in a small saucepan over low heat, without boiling, until sugar dissolves. Bring to the boil; boil, uncovered, without stirring, for 10 minutes or until thickened slightly and reaches 116°C/240°F on a sugar (candy) thermometer. Syrup should be thick but not coloured. Remove from heat, allow bubbles to subside. Beat egg whites in a small bowl with an electric mixer until soft peaks form. While motor is operating, add hot syrup in a thin steady stream; beat on high speed for 10 minutes or until mixture is thick.

CANDIED LEMON PEEL Using a vegetable peeler, remove rind thinly from lemons; cut into long thin strips. Stir sugar, the water and rind in a small saucepan over low heat, without boiling, until sugar dissolves. Bring to the boil. Reduce heat; simmer, uncovered, without stirring, for 5 minutes or until mixture is syrupy.

TOP TIPS ●

The cake can be made a day ahead; store, covered, in an airtight container. Assemble just before serving.

COOKIES & CREAM ICE-CREAM CAKE

Perfect for summer sweets, you can use any ice-cream you like for this recipe, adding your favourite chocolate bar or lollies for a new twist.

INGREDIENTS

1 litre (4 cups) vanilla soy ice-cream

1 litre (4 cups) chocolate soy ice-cream

COOKIE DOUGH

125g (4 ounces) dairy-free spread

⅓ cup (75g) firmly packed brown sugar

⅓ cup (75g) caster (superfine) sugar

1¼ cups (210g) gluten-free plain (all-purpose) flour

½ teaspoon bicarbonate of soda (baking soda)

125g (4 ounces) dairy-free dark chocolate, chopped coarsely

TOP TIPS

Use your favourite ice-creams for this recipe. You can add chopped chocolate bars, jubes, marshmallows or coconut to the ice-cream. Dairy-free chocolate is free from milk solids; choose a 75% cocoa chocolate and always read the packaging labels to ensure the brand of chocolate you buy is actually dairy-free.

INFO				SERVES 8
PREP + COOK TIME	40 MINUTES (+ FREEZING, COOLING & REFRIGERATION)			

HEALTH FACTOR	GLUTEN FREE	DAIRY FREE	NUT FREE	YEAST FREE	EGG FREE

FAT	ENERGY	CARB	PROTEIN	FIBRE
14.1g (3g sat)	1162kJ (397 cal)	64.6g	3.4g	3.2g

PER SERVING

METHOD

1 Make cookie dough; refrigerate for 30 minutes.

2 Preheat oven to 200°C/400°F. Grease and line a baking tray with baking paper.

3 Using a quarter of the dough, roll tablespoons into balls; place balls on tray, about 2cm (¾-inch) apart. Bake for 20 minutes or until browned lightly and firm. Cool on tray.

4 Blend or process biscuits until fine; store in an airtight container until needed.

5 Line a deep 20cm (8-inch) round cake pan with plastic wrap.

6 Slightly soften vanilla soy ice-cream. Cut the remaining cookie dough into chunks. Fold half the dough through the vanilla ice-cream; spoon into pan. Cover with foil; freeze for 30 minutes or until just firm.

7 Slightly soften chocolate soy ice-cream. Stir remaining cookie dough through chocolate ice-cream; spoon on vanilla ice-cream layer. Smooth surface, cover with foil; freeze for 3 hours or overnight.

8 Turn ice-cream cake upside-down onto a serving plate. Wipe side and base of pan with a warm cloth to release ice-cream from the pan; discard plastic wrap. Smooth ice-cream with a warm palette knife. Return to freezer for 30 minutes.

9 Just before serving, sprinkle top of ice-cream cake with reserved biscuit crumbs. Drizzle with extra melted dairy-free dark chocolate, if you like.

COOKIE DOUGH Beat dairy-free spread and sugars in a medium bowl with an electric mixer until pale. Beat in sifted flour and soda until smooth; stir in chocolate. Halve dough; wrap each half in plastic wrap.

CHRISTMAS FRUIT CAKE

Whether it's made as a gift or to serve after dinner, the festive season isn't complete without the fruity goodness of a traditional yuletide cake.

INGREDIENTS

dairy-free spread, for greasing

1kg (2 pounds) mixed dried fruit

½ cup (125ml) sweet sherry

250g (8 ounces) dairy-free spread

1¼ cups (250g) firmly packed brown sugar

½ cup (125ml) soy milk

1¼ cups (170g) gluten-free plain (all-purpose) flour

1 cup (65g) gluten-free baby rice cereal

½ cup (75g) 100% corn (maize) cornflour (cornstarch)

½ teaspoon bicarbonate of soda (baking soda)

1 teaspoon ground cinnamon

3 eggs, beaten lightly

METHOD

1 Preheat oven to 150°C/300°F. Grease a deep 20cm (8-inch) round cake pan with dairy-free spread; line base and side with three layers of baking paper, extending the papers 5cm (2 inches) above the side.

2 Combine fruit and half the sherry in a large bowl.

3 Stir dairy-free spread, sugar and milk in a medium saucepan over low heat until sugar is dissolved and spread is melted; pour over fruit mixture. Stir sifted dry ingredients into fruit mixture, in two batches, until combined. Stir in egg.

4 Spread mixture evenly into pan. Tap pan firmly on the bench to settle the mixture; smooth the surface.

5 Bake cake for 2½ hours or until cooked when tested (insert the blade of a sharp pointed knife gently through the centre of the cake to the bottom of the pan; gently withdraw the knife, there should be no uncooked mixture on the blade). If necessary, cover the cake with foil during cooking to prevent over-browning.

6 Brush hot cake with remaining sherry. Cover hot cake with foil; cool in pan overnight.

INFO

SERVES 12

PREP + COOK TIME 3 HOURS (+ COOLING)				

HEALTH FACTOR	GLUTEN FREE	DAIRY FREE	NUT FREE	

FAT	ENERGY	CARB	PROTEIN	FIBRE
17.4g (4.1g sat)	2244kJ (536 cal)	145.4g	4.5g	4.8g

PER SERVING

TOP TIPS

Replace the sherry with orange juice, if you prefer. The cake can be made up to 2 weeks ahead; store in an airtight container in the refrigerator, or freeze for up to 3 months.

GLOSSARY

Almonds
flaked paper-thin slices.
meal almonds ground to a coarse flour texture.
slivered small pieces cut lengthways.

Bacon rashes also called bacon slices.

Baking powder a raising agent; consists of two parts cream of tartar to one part bicarbonate of soda. Gluten-free baking powder is made without cereals.

Brazil nuts a triangular-shelled oily nut with an unusually tender white flesh and a mild, rich flavour.

Butter use salted or unsalted (sweet); 125g is equal to one stick (4 ounces) butter

Buttermilk is commercially made like yoghurt; sold alongside dairy products in supermarkets.

Cheese
cream commonly called Philadelphia or Philly, a soft cow milk cheese with a fat content of at least 33%. Sold at supermarkets in bulk and packaged.
fetta Greek in origin; a crumbly goat's- or sheep-milk cheese with a sharp, salty taste.
mascarpone an Italian fresh cultured-cream product made like yoghurt. White to creamy yellow with a buttery-rich texture. Soft, creamy and spreadable.
parmesan hard, grainy cow's-milk cheese.
pizza a commercial blend of varying proportions of grated mozzarella, cheddar and parmesan.
ricotta a sweet, moist, soft, white, cow's-milk cheese; slightly grainy texture.

Chicken tenderloins thin strip of meat under the breast

Chocolate
Choc Melts small discs of compounded milk, white or dark chocolate, ideal for melting and moulding.
dark eating (70% cocoa solids) also called semi-sweet; made of a high percentage of cocoa liquor and cocoa butter, and little added sugar. We use dark eating chocolate unless stated otherwise.
white eating contains no cocoa solids, deriving its sweetness from cocoa butter. Very sensitive to heat.

Cinnamon dried inner bark of the shoots of the cinnamon tree; comes in sticks (quills) and ground; one of the world's most common spices, used universally as a sweet, fragrant flavouring for both sweet and savoury foods.

Cloves dried flower buds of a tropical tree; can be used whole or ground. They have a strong scent and taste so should be used sparingly.

Cocoa powder also called unsweetened cocoa.

Coconut
cream obtained commercially from the first pressing of the coconut flesh alone, without added water; the second pressing is sold as coconut milk. Available in supermarkets.
desiccated concentrated, dried, unsweetened and finely shredded coconut flesh.
flaked dried flaked coconut flesh. shredded unsweetened thin strips of dried coconut.

Coriander
fresh also called cilantro; bright-green-leafed herb with a pungent flavour.

Cornflakes, gluten-free available from health food stores or the health food section in supermarkets.

Cream we use fresh pouring cream (pure cream).
sour thick, commercially-cultured sour cream with at least 35% fat content.
thickened a whipping cream containing thickener. Has at least 35% fat content.

Cream of tartar acid ingredient in baking powder; used in confectionery mixtures to help prevent sugar from crystallising.

Cucumber
lebanese short, slender and thin-skinned. Probably the most popular variety because of its fresh and flavoursome taste.
telegraph also known as the european or cucumber; long and slender with shallow ridges running down the length of its thin dark-green skin.

Cumin has a spicy, nutty flavour. Available in seed, dried and ground form.

Currants dried tiny, almost black raisins so-named from the grape type native to Corinth, Greece.

Dates fruit of the date palm tree, eaten fresh or dried. About 4cm to 6cm in length, oval and plump; honey-sweet in flavour with a sticky texture.

Dill used fresh or dried, as seeds or ground. Its feathery, frond-like fresh leaves are grassier and more subtle than the dried version or the seeds. Has an anise/celery sweetness.

Dried cranberries dried sweetened cranberries.

Eggs we use large chicken eggs weighing an average of 60g unless stated otherwise in the recipes in this book. If a recipe calls for raw or barely cooked eggs, exercise caution if there is a salmonella problem in your area, particularly in food eaten by children and pregnant women.

Flour
bread mix, gluten-free a commercial gluten-free bread mix available from most supermarkets.
buckwheat not a true cereal, but flour is made from its seeds. Available from health food stores.
chickpea also called besan or gram; made from ground chickpeas so is gluten-free and high in protein. Available from health food stores and the health food section in most supermarkets.
plain all-purpose flour made from wheat. Also available gluten-free from most supermarkets.
potato made from cooked potatoes which have been dried and ground.
rice very fine, almost powdery, gluten-free flour; made from ground white rice.
self-raising plain flour mixed with baking powder in the proportion of 1 cup flour to 2 teaspoons baking powder. Also available gluten-free from most supermarkets.
soya flour made from ground soya beans.

Garam masala literally meaning blended spices; based on varying proportions of cardamom, cinnamon, cloves, coriander, fennel and cumin, roasted and ground together.

Gelatine we use powdered gelatine. Also available in sheet form known as leaf gelatine.

Glacé fruit when buying glacé fruit check the ingredients label for 'glucose made from wheat' – glacé fruit is available without glucose, making it gluten-free and wheat-free.

Glacé ginger fresh ginger root preserved in sugar syrup; crystallised ginger can be substituted if rinsed with warm water and dried before use.

Gluten-free baking powder used as a leavening agent in bread, cake, pastry or pudding mixtures. Suitable for people with an allergic response to glutens or seeking an alternative to everyday baking powder. *see also* baking powder

Hazelnut meal hazelnuts ground to a coarse flour.

Kumara orange-fleshed sweet potato often confused with yam.

Linseed meal ground linseed (flax seeds). Available from health food stores and supermarkets.

Linseed, sunflower and almond meal (LSA) available from health food stores and in the health food section at supermarkets.

Macadamias a rich, buttery nut. Has a high oil content so should be stored in the refrigerator.

Mandarin also called tangerine; a small, loose-skinned, easy-to-peel, sweet and juicy citrus fruit. Mandarin juice is available in the refrigerated section in supermarkets.

Milk
we use full-cream milk, unless otherwise specified.
buttermilk in spite of its name, buttermilk is actually low in fat, varying between 0.6 per cent and 2.0 per cent per 100ml. It is readily available from the dairy department in supermarkets. Because it is low in fat, it's a good substitute for dairy products such as cream or sour cream in baking and dressings.
evaporated unsweetened canned milk from which water has been extracted by evaporation. Evaporated skim or low-fat milk has 0.3 per cent fat content.
full-cream powder instant powdered milk made from whole cow milk with liquid removed and emulsifiers added.
sweetened condensed a canned milk product consisting of milk with more than half the water content removed and sugar added to the remaining milk.

Mixed peel candied citrus peel, usually consisting of orange and lemon peel.

Pancetta an Italian unsmoked bacon; pork belly cured in salt and spices then rolled into a sausage shape and dried for several weeks.

Peanuts also known as groundnut, not in fact a nut but the pod of a legume. We mainly use raw (unroasted) or unsalted roasted peanuts.

Pecans golden brown, buttery, rich nut; walnuts are a good substitute. Also available in pieces.

Pistachios green, delicately flavoured nuts inside hard off-white shells. Available salted or unsalted in their shells.

Polenta also called cornmeal; a flour-like cereal made of corn (maize). Also the dish made from it.

Poppy seeds small, dried, bluish-grey seeds; crunchy and nutty. Available whole or ground from delicatessens and most supermarkets.

Pure maple syrup distilled from the sap of maple trees. Maple-flavoured syrup or pancake syrup is not an adequate substitute for the real thing.

Rice flakes, gluten-free available from the health food section in most supermarkets.

Rice, rolled flattened rice grain rolled into flakes; looks similar to rolled oats.

Shallots also called french shallots, golden shallots or eschalots. Small and elongated, with a brown-skin, they grow in tight clusters similar to garlic.

Silver beet also called swiss chard and mistakenly called spinach; a member of the beet family grown for its tasty green leaves and celery-like stems. Best cooked rather than eaten raw.

Skewers metal or bamboo skewers can be used. Rub oil onto metal skewers to stop meat sticking; soak bamboo skewers in water for at least 1 hour or overnight to prevent them splintering or scorching during cooking.

Spinach also called english spinach and incorrectly, silver beet. Best eaten raw in salads; the larger leaves should be added last to soups, stews and stir-fries, and should be cooked until barely wilted.

Sterilising jars it's important your hands, the preparation area, tea towels and cloths etc, are clean. Always start with cleaned washed jars and lids, then follow one of these methods:
(1) Put the jars and lids through the hottest cycle of a dishwasher without using any detergent; or
(2) Stand the jars upright, without touching each other, on a wooden board on the lowest shelf in the oven. Turn the oven to the lowest possible temperature, close the oven door and leave the jars to heat through for 30 minutes.

Remove the jars from the oven or dishwasher with a towel. Stand the jars upright and not touching each other on a wooden board, or a bench covered with a clean towel to protect and insulate the bench. Fill the jars as instructed.

Sugar
brown an extremely soft, finely granulated sugar retaining molasses for its colour and flavour.
caster also called superfine or finely granulated table sugar. The fine crystals dissolve easily.
pure icing also known as confectioners' sugar or powdered sugar.
white a coarse, granulated table sugar, also called crystal sugar.

Sultanas (golden raisins) dried seedless white grapes.

Tahini sesame seed paste available from Middle Eastern food stores.

Tofutti a tofu-based dairy-free cream cheese substitute, available in the refrigerated section of health food stores and major supermarkets.

Turmeric also called kamin; related to galangal and ginger. Must be grated or pounded to release its pungent flavour. Fresh turmeric can be substituted with the more common dried powder.

Vanilla
bean dried, long, thin pod from a tropical golden orchid; the minuscule black seeds inside the bean are used to impart a luscious vanilla flavour.
extract obtained from vanilla beans infused in water; a non-alcoholic version of essence.

Watercress a peppery salad green; highly perishable, use as soon as possible after purchase.

Xantham Gum is a thickening agent produced by fermentation of, usually, corn sugar. When buying Xanthan gum, ensure the packet states 'made from fermented corn sugar'. Found in the health-food section in most larger supermarkets

Yeast a raising agent used in dough making. Granular (7g sachets) and fresh compressed (20g blocks) of yeast can usually be substituted for each other.

Yoghurt we use plain full-cream yoghurt in our recipes unless noted otherwise. If a recipe in this book calls for low-fat yoghurt, we use one with a fat content of less than 0.2 per cent.
Greek-style plain yoghurt that has been strained in a cloth (traditionally muslin) to remove the whey and to give it a creamy consistency. It is ideal for use in dips and dressings.

Zucchini also called courgette; belongs to the squash family. Yellow flowers can be stuffed or used in salads.

INDEX

Published in 2016 by Bounty Books based on material licensed to it by Bauer Media Books, Australia.

Bauer Media Books is a division of Bauer Media Pty Limited, 54 Park St, Sydney; GPO Box 4088, Sydney, NSW 2001, Australia
phone (+61) 2 9282 8618; fax (+61) 2 9126 3702
www.awwcookbooks.com.au

BAUER MEDIA BOOKS
PUBLISHER Jo Runciman
EDITORIAL & FOOD DIRECTOR Pamela Clark
DIRECTOR OF SALES, MARKETING & RIGHTS Brian Cearnes
CREATIVE DIRECTOR Hannah Blackmore
EDITOR Erin Mayo
FOOD EDITOR Rebecca Meli
SENIOR DESIGNER Meng Koach
OPERATIONS MANAGER David Scotto

Published and distributed in the United Kingdom by Bounty Books, a division of Octopus Publishing Group Ltd
Carmelite House
50 Victoria Embankment
London, EC4Y 0DZ
United Kingdom
info@octopusbooks.co.uk;
www.octopusbooks.co.uk

PRINTED BY Leo Paper Products Ltd, China.

INTERNATIONAL FOREIGN LANGUAGE RIGHTS
Brian Cearnes, Bauer Media Books
bcearnes@bauer-media.com.au

A catalogue record for this book is available from the British Library.
ISBN: 978-0-7537-3128-4
© Bauer Media Pty Limited 2016
ABN 18 053 273 546

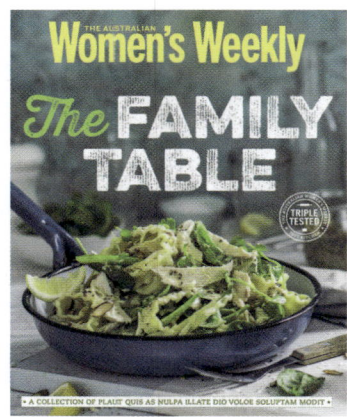